BEAR TRACKS

*The Development of the Repo
Strip Market at Bear Stearns*

DAVID S. MARREN

ISBN: 1500736244
ISBN 13: 9781500736248

The proceeds from this book will help fund research of Primary Lateral Sclerosis (PLS), an upper motor neuron disease, at Columbia University Medical Center. If a reader wants to make a tax-deductible donation to help fund PLS research, I would be most appreciative. Kindly make checks payable to The Trustees of Columbia University, indicate David S. Marren PLS Research Fund on the memo line, and mail to the following address:

Columbia University Medical Center
Office of Development
Attention: Matt Reals
100 Haven Avenue, Suite 29D
New York, NY 10032

DEDICATION

*To Dr. Debra Adler-Klein, Dr. Amiram Katz, and Dr. Hiroshi Mitsumoto
and his staff at Columbia University Medical Center.
I don't know where I would be without you.*

ACKNOWLEDGMENTS

My heartfelt thanks –

To the many good people I met at Bear Stearns over the years, especially those on the Finance Desk.

To Tim, who was my partner at Bear Stearns and friend for over twenty-five years.

To my many friends in Darien, Connecticut.

To my Stackloaf brethren, it definitely shows that FIJI is not for college days alone.

To the constant support from Mark and Chet.

To Chris, for helping me on my journey.

To Al and Mark, for giving me a great gift.

To Beth, for providing a guiding hand.

To Susie and Bill, for all your help.

To my siblings, for always being there for me.

To my parents, Bernard and Ellen, for showing me there is always a "right way" to do things, whether you like it or not.

To my children, for the joy I have received from watching you grow up.

To my wonderful wife, Caroline, who has been with me every step of the way.

I started writing this book to raise money for Primary Lateral Sclerosis. As I wrote, it occurred to me that my life story was a real tribute to my parents. Determination, honesty, and hard work are not taught in a textbook, they are learned at an early age and remain with you forever. This became apparent as I looked back at my professional and personal life. It is the real measure of success. I can only hope my children learn as much from me as I have learned from my parents.

In memory of
Bernard and Ellen Marren

TABLE OF CONTENTS

INTRODUCTION

THOUGHTS

MARCH 14, 2008

Little did I or my fellow fourteen thousand employees know this would be Bear Stearns' final day. Our stock had been plummeting, but I knew our earnings were coming out in a few days; they were going to be a pleasant surprise, and that would satisfy some people. Here is what transpired that morning.

At about 7:30 a.m. on Friday, March 14, the employees of the Finance Desk were called into Paul Friedman's office. Paul, my boss and the chief administration officer in fixed income, had been at the office all night and was very tired but elated. He told us there was going to be an announcement later that morning that Bear Stearns was going to use the Federal Reserve window at JPMorgan Chase, making the Federal Reserve our lender of last resort. Our excess cash position had been drawn down—it had gone from $17 billion on Tuesday to $2 billion now. With that problem and others, the Federal Reserve had given us a lifeline. They would fund our position for up to twenty-eight days with the help of JPMorgan Chase, our clearing bank.

Senior management thought we had new life; both my partner Tim Greene and I thought differently (Tim and I were co-heads of the Finance Desk). The mere fact that we could not stand on our own two feet but had to rely on someone else was going to be very detrimental in the marketplace. The only good thing about the meeting with Paul was that we felt we could ethically do business with our customers before the announcement. By 8:30 a.m., our entire funding obligation was done. At 8:45 a.m. the announcement came; after the announcement, we started fielding phone calls from major customers. A few wanted to back out of trades done earlier that day, so we let them. We really didn't care because we had a backstop. Most customers allowed the trades to stand. The customers who backed out of trades had high-quality collateral for the most part, so we traded some of that collateral on the broker screen. The customers didn't care what the collateral was—they just didn't want our name on their books.

As the morning went on, every funding source said they would not trade with us on Monday. We ended up using about $5 billion of the facility that day. After having a brief rally from $60 to $65, our stock traded lower all day, closing at about $30. We were doomed.

JULY 9, 2014

I know a husband should only think about his wife on their anniversary (I have been happily married to Caroline for twenty-six years), but this day is memorable in another way. Chris Milhous, a very good friend from college, asked me a question I've never been asked before: "Assuming other sophisticated investors accept the existing 1099 process for interest income on STRIPS, have you ever calculated the lost IRS revenue?" The answer is no, so these are only my guesses, but given my professional and personal experiences with STRIPS, I believe they are close approximations. The market for STRIPS has been growing steadily since being introduced in 1985. Today it is now over $200 billion in size and growing. In my opinion, since 1985 the federal government has lost approximately $45 billion in uncollected taxes, and over the next five years, it will lose at least an additional $14 billion if it doesn't fix the problem.

Here is my full story.

BEFORE THE FINANCE DESK

ROAD TO THE FINANCE DESK

Growing up in an Irish Catholic, middle-class family in White Plains, New York, I assumed everyone grew up the same way. Based on the teachings of my loving parents, who valued religion, education, and a close-knit family, I figured if people were smart and worked hard, they would get ahead. I wasn't right or wrong, but I did leave out one very important aspect that, unfortunately, we did not have—connections. My mother always said, "The hardest part was getting in. Once in, the cream always rises to the top."

As the fifth of six children, I was blessed with a few things. Although smart, particularly in math, I was near the bottom of my family in terms of academics; however, I was at the top in athletics. I was captain of many teams, enhancing my leadership capabilities. I excelled at all sports. I was big for my age, so I had an advantage right from the beginning. Although I did eventually stop growing, I still played football and baseball in college. My father died suddenly of cancer between my junior and senior year in college and I had to figure out what I was going to do with my life.

When my first big break came, I didn't even know it. Since I loved sports and had learned a good work ethic from my parents, at age 12 I began caddying at Metropolis Country Club, which was near our home. I worked myself from a "rabbit" (who carried only one bag) to the number-one summer caddy over a ten-year period, carrying double bags eleven rounds per week.

Caddying was hard work but very lucrative. I always had a chart on my bedroom wall, counting my rounds, and put a significant amount of money in the bank. I didn't think this was profound, just normal—I was a saver.

After a few years, I caddied for the same foursome (Al Sarnoff, Billy Kay, Chuck Benwitt, and Robert Julius) every weekend. They were very good golfers as well as nice people. They even took another caddy and me with them on their vacation to upstate New York. They were very protective of me when my father passed away. When I graduated from college in 1983, a member of the foursome arranged an interview for me at Bear Stearns. I got the job in their operations training program, making the huge sum of $14,000 per year. I also learned about taxes. The $14,000 quickly became less, as opposed to caddying. Although ecstatic, I continued working for a few years as a caddy on the weekends to augment my salary.

My starting date was September 6, 1983. Little did I know this would be the birth date of my first child eight years later and would mark the beginning of another saga. In those days the operations training program was for recent college graduates, who worked in the "cage," a secure location that would process the equity trades done at the firm. Processing trades included anything operationally from trade date to settlement date (trade date + 3 days). It used to be 5 days when it was even more manual.

While I enjoyed working in Operations and learned a lot about the mechanics of trading, I was anxious to move to a more challenging position within the bank. Members of the operations training program were in a pool of people to be considered if an immediate job opening occurred in a growing area of the firm. It was a brilliant strategy, since Wall Street was expanding, and a start in operations gave insight into most divisions. In addition, it provided potential upward mobility because those in the lower ranks could see fellow employees advance, building loyalty. The CEO liked individuals who were PSD: poor, smart, and had a deep desire to become successful. I liked the place already.

As a recent college graduate, one of my frequent activities outside of work involved weekend road trips to visit friends. After three social events in four weeks, all I wanted to do was to get a weekend of sleep but this was when my second break came. I was invited to a bachelor party in Southern New Jersey. The groom's father and Bill Schreyer were there. Bill Schreyer was the CEO of Merrill Lynch. There was another good friend of mine in attendance, who was also in the Bear Stearns training program. We both chatted with Bill, and he said he knew our CEO, Ace Greenberg, well and that Ace better watch it or he would steal us away. As my mother said, "You never get a second chance to make a first impression."

By Monday morning we had forgotten all about Saturday night, but that was about to change. At 8:50 a.m. I got a phone call from Ace Greenberg, who asked if my friend and I could come right down to his desk on the equity-trading floor. Ace had received a phone call from his friend, Bill, who had told him about two up-and-coming stars who were working at Bear Stearns. I was going on internal interviews shortly thereafter.

Vinny Mattone was a gruff, street-smart individual. He had come to the firm with Bill Michaelcheck from Salomon Brothers a few years earlier to start the fixed-income business at Bear Stearns. Bill ran the Government Trading Desk, and Vinny ran the Government Finance Desk. Vinny gave me my third break. During my interview, the main item that Vinny focused on was not my good grades or leadership capabilities, but that I was living at home with my widowed mother. He saw this dedication to family as my most important asset, since the Finance Desk at Bear Stearns was his "family." I got the job and started in May 1984.

As my mother would tell me, "Remember, breaks don't just happen—they are earned."

THE EARLY YEARS

THE FINANCE DESK

The Fixed Income Finance Desk performs many different functions including funding the firm and covering the firm shorts. In the beginning, most securities were issued by the United States Government. Treasury bills were issued weekly and matured in periods less than 1 year. Some treasury notes were issued monthly but most were issued quarterly and matured in periods up to 10 years. Treasury bonds, the longest debt instrument, were issued quarterly (February 15, May 15, August 15, and November 15) and matured in 20 or 30 years. By the end, over 25 years many things evolve and different types of securities were added to the mix.

Within funding, there were three distinct areas: specials, off-the-run specials, and general collateral. Specials were current issues – bills, notes, bonds and usually the prior current issue. They changed often and were the majority of trades; off-the-run specials were any issues Bear Stearns had a need for or another dealer had a need for; and general collateral was when the counterparty did not care what we gave them—it just had to have the full faith and credit of the US Treasury. Although funding the firm's trading position is the top priority of the Finance Desk, the Finance Desk made money through its matchbook activities. Reverse repos and repos of the same issue (usually specials) are matched and for the most part the daily interest rate spread differential generated a profit.

"Finance Desk" is also sometimes called the "repo desk." Repo (short for repurchase agreement) is the delivery of securities and receipt of cash. Most repo trades started one day and ended the next day: even if they were written as open, the trades were really overnight, and the rate was negotiated each day. If the rate was not agreed upon by both parties, the trade was closed. Repo is a same-day business. Every repo can be thought of as a sell, and every reverse repo could be thought of as a buy. Every ticket (repo or reverse repo) had the counterparty (which we denoted by the short name), issue, price, and end date (overnight, open, or to a specific date). Every day, the various traders' jobs were to get each position to zero. All the longs (repos) had to be funded (lowest rate), and all the shorts (reverse repos) had to be covered (highest rate).

My job when I arrived on the Finance Desk was to manually post trades to T accounts (repos and reverse repos) while sitting at a lunch table, facing a wall. The T accounts were the start-of-day position of every issue, and I posted any changes. Each account had a coded name. Whoever thought up these names should have had his or her head examined. A few "short" names were longer than the original account names! It was tedious work but nevertheless important. The individual who had held my job previously mixed up a certain maturity of Treasury bills with the same maturity of Bear Stearns partners' bills, which were also the same Treasury bill but had their own line. This was capital and profits Bear Stearns had built up and invested very conservatively. These bills could never be mixed up; they were priceless. We ate lunch at our desks every day and given that the firm was located at 55 Water Street in downtown Manhattan, two of my favorite delis were Taste Buds and Marc Franks.

One of the things my parents always preached about was the importance of education. Upon my father's passing, my mother worked at Pace University, where children of employees could attend for free. I enrolled in their evening division of the Business School and got my

Masters of Business Administration. Around the same time, in June 1984, Bear Stearns hired Tim Greene for the Finance Desk. Tim had started in the cage with me, and he and I would later be promoted to co-heads of the Finance Desk. Imagine that—two Irish guys at a predominantly Jewish firm. It was all about profitability. Tim and I would face that wall together.

In those days I was glad when I had school, because I would get home at 11:00 p.m. When I didn't have school, I often didn't get home until midnight. I was at my desk every morning at 6:30 a.m. We would always joke about others. If you howled at night, you had to sing in the morning. Work was Monday to Friday, rarely any weekends (as opposed to much later, when I thought about it 24/7, even though I was only there on weekdays). As a MBA finance major, the economic classes I took made a lot more sense.

To work on the Finance Desk each one of us had to pass the Series 7 exam to get a federal license and the Series 63 to get a state license. These were not difficult tests, but were demanding and we were expected to pass. 70 percent was a pass, and 69 percent was a fail. Tim and I had different ways of preparing for these tests. I spent a lot of time studying and did very well. Tim looked at the material for a very short time and did well. Tim told me I wasted a lot of effort.

During the mid-1980s, on a daily basis at about 1:30 p.m., Tim would put on his mortgage-clearing hat and finance the new type of securities—mortgages. At that time we cleared treasuries at Manufacturers Hanover and mortgages at Morgan Bank. That would change.

TRADING AND OPERATIONS

The key to a successful career on the Finance Desk was to develop good relationships with the Government Trading Desk as well as the Operations area. When I started on the Finance Desk, I knew very little about either area. The Government Trading Desk consisted of about 15-20 people. They had a specific timeframe of securities they were responsible for (0 - 1 year, 1 year - 2 years, 2 years - 4 years, etc.). There were a few sales people as well who covered large, active, accounts. Every Government trade flowed to us the subsequent day. From my days in the Cage, I knew that after traders did a trade, they assumed the delivery process would go smoothly and went quickly on to their next trades. The Finance Desk knew that operationally, it didn't always happen that way.

The Operations area was our voice to our clearing bank, JPMorgan Chase (which was Manufacturers Hanover at the time). Employees in operations were located about ten feet away from the Finance Desk, and we had access to them through a window in the wall, which was always open. They had to be nearby in case we had to yell instructions to them. This was how sophisticated fixed income was in 1984. Some very knowledgeable people who were vital to the Finance Desk's success were in operations, including Terrence Cregg, Joe Newman, Mike Boulos, and others.

When Tim and I were first hired, Bill Lee, an operational person who worked on the computer system, was later one of my mentors, and had been with Vinny at Salomon Brothers, told us to say hello to Bill Michaelcheck, the head of the Government Trading Desk. Since we didn't know who Bill was at the time and we were working very long days, we never said hello. Bill Lee asked us both about three months later if we had ever said hello to Bill. We said no and asked who he was. Bill Lee told us. We had blown it.

In our early years on the desk, Tim and I were always invited for cocktails at Harry's of Hanover Square by the Government Trading Desk. The desk senior people included Don Ross, Matt McCaffrey, and Eddie Williams. One of their broker friends was John Kenney. He looked like Barney Rubble from *The Flintstones* cartoon. He was also the funniest man I'd ever met. These people made Tim and me feel like family. We never paid for a beer for the longest time. One of my favorite memories was from Harry himself. If it was someone's birthday, he would swirl his finger at the bartender and say, "Buy the boys a round." It was always somebody's birthday.

During one particular Super Bowl, Mike Boulos had a party. Tim had entered a Super Bowl pool. A safety (holding in the end zone—a very rare occurrence) made Tim a big winner.

Eddie Williams was the bill trader and head trader on the Government Trading Desk. He was a great guy who died way too early. However, he was the victim of the greatest joke I ever witnessed. On a Thursday Eddie was out for dinner and started talking to a group at an adjacent table. Eddie offered them a tour of the Federal Reserve. The following morning Eddie got a call from the man at last night's adjacent table (it was really his assistant, Jim White). Eddie asked him if he wanted a tour, but instead the caller got mad and said that Eddie had fondled his wife's leg at dinner last night. The caller also said he was on his way over to beat Eddie up. Eddie told Tom Parker (another senior trader on the trading desk, who was in on the joke) to meet him in the hall. Tom told Eddie he should call the cops. He thought Eddie was going to have a heart attack right there. He then told Eddie about the joke.

CREDIT AND EXPOSURE

"Where is the AGNUM?" Bernadette Kelly would yell. I had no idea what it stood for, but it was important. It had all the trading desk positions, and she had to assign a rate for the day.

The exposure report monitored each counterparty. The report would lump all trades with each account, and it was reviewed every day. Due to daily price movements and changes, an account looked different each day. We had to take into account repos and reverse repos, overnight, open, and margin requirements at the start-of-term trades (which could be different on multiple issue types) with each account (the general rule on term trades was a one-quarter-point margin per month). If the account was "in deficit", we called the account for margin—we had to do this by 10:00 a.m. If we were "in deficit", they would call us—but we hoped they wouldn't.

There was a whole method associated with this besides just exposure. Repricing a trade had costs associated with it, plus the interest on the trade would be "cleaned up" when we repriced. We wanted to get paid the interest on money given to a counterparty, but we didn't want to pay interest if we didn't have to. When we met our exposure with margin collateral, it had a ticket cost but no interest ramifications. This small detail was profitable as the numbers got larger. We would reprice an issue if the counterparty owed more than $500,000 in interest—this sounds like a lot but was obtained if sizes were big and rates were high. We didn't earn interest on the interest—only on the principal—but we factored the interest into the margin. In the beginning this was relatively straightforward to manage, as the pricing was very easy to obtain and most items were treasuries. This would get harder in later years, as the price was not as easily obtained. We had nine ways to price mortgages, from simple feeds to matrix pricing to trader pricing. It was a very time-consuming process, but it was vital.

Every so often the Finance Desk would wire the fixed-income profits to the Treasury Department. After several years and bigger profits, this became a monthly occurrence. Managing our cash and collateral was a precise job. Despite this "loss of cash", we had to manage both efficiently. It was important to realize the interest on our trades.

The Finance Desk could make money in all types of interest-rate environments, since the bulk of what we did was short term. The Federal Reserve was responsible for any changes in interest-rate policy. Lower interest rates were thought to spur the economy, while higher rates were thought to slow the economy. To use a car analogy, lower rates were like tapping the accelerator, while higher rates were like touching the brakes. When rates were falling, the Finance Desk made the most money.

Security lenders were covered by every dealer. They were the trust side of every major commercial bank. If a bank had a big account, it would put its treasuries out to the dealer community and then reinvest the proceeds in a variety of assets. This would create a sizeable spread. Security lenders split the proceeds with the account, although the split spread changed over time. The goal was to consistently get as many issues out as possible. This would allow the security lender to make a big profit.

THE FEDWIRE

The Fedwire was the simultaneous delivery of a security and payment of cash. The Finance Desk conducted the majority of business on the Fedwire. Bear Stearns was a primary dealer. It was open for primary dealer–to–primary dealer deliveries from 9:00 a.m. until 2:30 p.m. or later—fifteen minutes later for primary dealer–to–customer trades and fifteen more minutes of reversal. The closing of the Fedwire was a crucial time of the day. The most important lessons I learned were about fails to deliver (FTD) and fails to receive (FTR). If we didn't have to pay out money (FTR) but could make all our deliveries, we would get to reinvest that cash overnight. A $1 million fail was equal to about twenty-seven dollars times the prevailing interest rate. A $100 million trade was one hundred times more valuable. To put it simply, if a person owed $100 to AT&T for a phone bill, he or she wouldn't care if the check was cashed today or tomorrow, but if the check was for $100 million, he or she would care. The more net FTRs (as opposed to FTDs) we achieved, the better.

There were a few issues that were not eligible to be wired. We bought premise (or hold-in custody) money from customers, and they took our valuation. In later years we funded much of our position through tri-party repo (see page 81 for more detail). This money was sent to our clearing bank by our customer, and we assigned collateral to the money. The money was for a certain type of collateral. Treasuries were "better" than STRIPS, which were "better" than mortgages. When we had fulfilled our obligation, our clearing bank released the money to us.

Although spreads got tighter over time, in 1984 they were about seventy-five basis points for specials and forty basis points for off-the-run specials (A basis point is defined as 1 percent of 1 percent so that 100 basis points is equivalent to 1 percent). The interest was earned daily. General collateral was traded around federal funds. Our job was to borrow securities (reverse repo) at the highest rate (earning high interest on our money) and lend securities (repo) at the lowest rate (paying low interest on their money), putting out as many specials as we could. The most important part of the Finance Desk day was from 8:00 to 10:00 a.m. and around the close of the Fedwire. The day was very busy, even more so in the eighties when many of the tasks were less computerized.

In my first few years on the Finance Desk, we could deliver any amount over the Fedwire (up to 999 million), and it made fails even more important. Later, the maximum size was reduced to 50 million. This made clearing easier but also increased the number of deliveries.

As I said earlier, the Fedwire could close at 2:30 p.m. but rarely did. On one occasion, many of the senior traders left to see a customer in Connecticut. They assured the remaining people that the Fedwire would be up for a long time. They were wrong—it closed at 2:30 that day. We scrambled and broke even. This was an amazing accomplishment for the B team. (Eventually, we would become the A team, but at this point we did not have enough experience.) We were very pleased with ourselves.

One of the funnier moments that ever occurred on the Finance Desk happened one day at the close of the Fedwire. Roberta Philmus covered specials and off-the-run specials during the 1980s. At the close of the Fedwire, we had to call our clearing bank directly to make a lot of last-second deliveries, which couldn't go through the normal process because there wasn't enough time. In this instance, Roberta instructed the bank to deliver one million of a security versus $1 million. The bank made the delivery of one million versus $1 billion, and the Fedwire closed. Although the bank made the mistake, it was Roberta's trade. Roberta had overdrawn the Bank of New York by $999 million. After a good laugh, it was worked out.

BORROWING AND DEBT

Vinny always preached about never having debt. He would say, "If you were on a street corner, would you rather be the person who needs $100 or the person with $100?" This was a simple concept, but a lot of people on Wall Street didn't get it. They went out and bought lavish homes, fancy cars, and other ostentatious items on credit. They thought the money was going to roll in forever. This was definitely not what Vinny or my parents taught me. Work hard and save your pennies. Debt was a nasty four-letter word.

At 11:00 a.m. every morning, the Finance Desk could borrow a position from the New York Federal Reserve, but only overnight. This was expensive and a last resort, but the Federal Reserve's open-market account owned almost every issue. It was a competitive bidding process, so we weren't guaranteed to get an issue. If we were going to them, we would always bid to win.

Over my years at Bear Stearns, I learned a very important lesson about the Finance Desk: Fridays were special. Although Friday was only 20 percent of the business week, it accounted for three days' worth of interest ($\approx$ 43 percent of the week's profits and losses). Long weekends such as Memorial Day, Labor Day, Martin Luther King Jr. Day, President's Day, Good Friday, Columbus Day, and other rotating holidays (July 4, Christmas Day, New Year's Day) were over 1 percent of the year and therefore extremely important. Due to federal laws in the United States, the federal system was allowed to be closed consecutively for a maximum of three days. We always wanted our A team (veteran traders who knew the business) there on Fridays and before long weekends. If we were going up against another dealer's A team, it was a dogfight; if we were going up against a B team (younger, less-seasoned people), it was usually a bloodbath. An example of this occurred during Hurricane Gloria. Vinny loved chaos. Most desks were sent home, but not ours. We collected over four hundred million FTRs. It was a very profitable day on the Bear Stearns Finance Desk. We were happy to survive the hurricane. Vinny was glad it was a Friday.

It was always very important to have our A team there for two reasons. One, we could take advantage of our competitors and perform the best job covering shorts and funding the firm. The second was similar to the first—we would be able to have a very profitable day for the Finance Desk's matchbook.

There were two departments involved in all the money in the firm; the Finance Desk and the Treasury Department. The Finance Desk controlled all fixed income, except the Municipal Department and Corporate bonds, and the Treasury was in charge of everything else in the firm including the equity business, the prime brokerage business, payroll and others.

There were two schools of thought regarding unsecured money. The more conservative view was to buy the best collateral with profits. This was how Bear Stearns did it when it was a partnership. If we needed to raise funds via that collateral, we could do it easily. The second school of thought was funding our worst collateral with unsecured money raised in the commercial paper market. Any profits made in Fixed Income would be transferred to the Bear Stearns Treasury Department. We would never buy collateral with those profits but just invest them in the company. This meant borrowing money on our company's name as opposed to the collateral. This was very profitable, but it would be difficult to use that collateral to raise funds when needed. In 2008 when we needed it, it wasn't there.

There was a direct relationship between collateral and money, and we could really see it at the end of the day. If the collateral was all spoken for, the money left should be equal to zero. Theoretically, this should be the case, but the Finance Desk dealt in reality. When this didn't happen we had to find out why. My first introduction to the firm account (every trading account was blended together so we saw one net position for each issue) was early in my time with Bear Stearns. Every repo and reverse repo was accounted for. There was even a sixteen-digit adding machine in operations that counted each money movement—positive and negative. As we got more products over the years, it got harder and harder to find the mistake, but there always was one.

Every so often the Federal Reserve would conduct open-market operations. They would inject or remove money from the banking system, primarily through overnight repos but occasionally through term repos or matched sales (by putting out Treasury bills they owned, effectively taking money out of the system). In my early years, the Federal Reserve hid their intentions much more, and these types of operations might signal a policy shift. By the end they would verbally communicate their intentions to change policy.

TECHNOLOGY

Everyone was in such a good mood. Little did I know it was bonus payday (year-end was April 30). The good mood quickly changed, and I found out how demanding a business it really was. Vinny was putting in a new computer system (it operated on the Finance Desk from 1987 to the JPMorgan Chase takeover). The goal of the computer system was to automate many of the time consuming manual tasks. It was state of the art but you needed to have a complete grasp of all the tasks it was automating. We worked on the computer system each night at 5:00 p.m. after the "normal daily activities" were done.

In 1986 Vinny was out sick. Another senior managing director, the head of fixed-income operations, explicitly instructed us not to input any trades into Vinny's computer system. I was in charge of the new computer system, and I knew Vinny would want us to input the trades, so we input them. The head of fixed-income operations was not happy. Vinny made me go down to his office and apologize. I was very close to being fired. Although it was wrong to disobey a senior managing director and Vinny would never say it, I believe he was extremely happy that someone had stood up for him in his absence. He probably protected me.

When we began to use Vinny's computer system, he came out of his office and did something I will never forget. He took the old T accounts, which were our bible, and threw them in the garbage, saying, "If anyone gets them out, they're fired." The new system was launched.

Vinny had a lot of ideas; nine out of ten would never come to fruition, but the tenth was usually a home run. That was the case with the Custodial Trust Company (CTC). CTC was a subsidiary of Bear Stearns. The firm had set up a clearing bank away from the money-center banks. The good news was it dramatically reduced costs, but the bad news was we were no longer a big fish at Manufacturers Hanover in the New York Federal Reserve District, which was the most prominent of the twelve Federal Reserve Districts. Instead, we were the only fish at the thinly capitalized CTC in the Philadelphia Federal Reserve District. This had advantages and disadvantages. We were now the biggest player in the Philadelphia Federal Reserve District, but we could no longer do the things we had taken for granted at Manufacturers Hanover. Being the only game in town, we got an early education in intraday overdrafts, which were similar to personal checking accounts but could not be overdrawn. Since each day our financing needs ended at zero and many trades were overnight, as securities came back the following day and we paid for them, our instructions had to be there to turn that collateral and get paid ourselves. In the 2000s New York banks started charging dealers for intraday overdrafts, and because of our CTC experience, we were well prepared.

CUSTOMERS

Prudential Insurance was a big account for Bear Stearns. Their lending desk was very important to us. The main people we talked to were Bob DeHaven, Andy DeRosa, and George O'Connor. We were all about the same age and grew up in the business. Bob would later go to Mitsui, Andy to Metropolitan Life, and George to Barclays Global Investors. They were all good men. We didn't go out very often, but when we did, something memorable usually happened. For example, Bob and Andy came to the Big East basketball tournament held in Madison Square Garden with Tim and me. We had tickets to both sessions (afternoon doubleheader and the evening doubleheader). We had about one and a half hours in between, just enough time for dinner. Before we sat down for dinner, Bob had enough excitement for one day and left.

Andy and some colleagues from Metropolitan Life went to a New York Rangers hockey game with us. The game ended and we ordered seven cars to take people home. It was a frigid night. Only three cars came immediately yet we waited outside for all of them to come. Why we didn't stay warm in the cars that were present, I will never know.

We also set up a touch football game near the Fourteenth Street power station with Metropolitan Life. There was very little grass on the field and plenty of rocks. During one play I fell down and cut my chin; it was bleeding enough to stop the game. I did not want to go to an emergency room. A good friend of mine from high school had married a doctor, so I decided to ask him to look at it. He gave me three stitches in his basement.

Later, George worked in San Francisco. His team would make an annual trip to New York to entertain their Wall Street clients. They always picked the best restaurants. Often, feeling very cosmopolitan, I would go to his chosen restaurant for a special occasion with my wife, Caroline.

The State Teachers Retirement System of Ohio was a huge account for Bear Stearns and in later years became an account for CTC. This was a real accomplishment for CTC and Bear Stearns. It was a great way for Bear Stearns to fund our mortgage position. We paid Ohio a fee—we gave them our mortgages and used their treasuries—and this kept our mortgage position in-house. We made a lot of money for Ohio and Bear Stearns, but despite saying they would never leave, they left. This turned out to be all right for Bear Stearns. Instead of having one large customer fully "locked up," we were forced to reinvent ourselves with many new accounts to fund our mortgage position. In the long run, it was better to have multiple accounts and have our mortgage position in the marketplace.

I remember two unique stories about customers. On a Saturday, we took a few customers to the Concord in the Catskills to play golf. There was a shot that was blind, but the competitive nature of the customer took over and he had scrambled up a tree (to see). After Tim and I became co-heads of the desk, we noticed a trader at Dreyfus was out sick for a very long time. We found out that he had donated a kidney to his sister. Although not a huge account for Bear Stearns, we were genuinely moved that someone could be so compassionate. Dreyfus could never do anything wrong as long as Tim and I were at Bear Stearns.

GOING PUBLIC

In 1987 Bear Stearns went public. The firm issued shares in an initial public offering, and partners who had a stake in the company already were given a similar amount of shares. They could sell them in the market, cashing out of their illiquid positions in the partnership. Some cashed out of most of their holdings, but many did not. Bear Stearns employees and their families were allowed to purchase shares at a discount. Many did. Employees held a majority of the shares. Bear Stearns was not the first to go public, nor would it be the last. I think it hurt Wall Street because it was now shareholder money not partner.

During the 1987 crash, Ace Greenberg did stand on his desk and swing a golf club to lighten the mood and show the employees that the world was not ending. Since the Federal Reserve controlled interest rates, they abruptly lowered rates to spur the economy after the crash. With the lowering of rates, the Finance Desk made a lot of money.

Those early years would create a good foundation of knowledge about the intricacies of the Finance Desk. The lessons I learned inputting a computer system could only have come by doing it manually.

Better input resulted in better output. This allowed me to know all aspects on the Finance Desk. Although Wall Street was a difficult place to work and there were many different managerial approaches, the beginning of my management style was emerging.

THE MIDDLE YEARS

STRIPS

As I became more experienced over the years, I really wanted something I could call my own. This led to my first foray into STRIPS in 1988. It began as a small opportunity, but I developed it into a large and profitable venture.

To understand this fixed-income instrument, you need to realize the source of the product. In 1985, due to investor demand, the US Treasury created "separate trading of interest and principal securities (STRIPS)", although STRIP became the terminology used most often and I will use them interchangeably.

STRIPS are a fixed-income security resulting from the separation of coupons and principal from the body of the security. STRIPS are sold at a significant discount to face value and offer no interest payments. They mature at par. The difference between the purchase price and the price redeemed at maturity is the investor's return. STRIPS can only be purchased from private brokers and dealers, not from the Federal Reserve or any governmental agency. STRIPS are created from existing US Treasury debt; it is not new debt issued by the government, just a change from already approved debt. Sophisticated investors do not want to deal with intervening coupons but want a lump sum at some future date. Holders do not receive interest from the government each year; rather, the investor agrees to pay taxes on the unearned interest of the STRIP for each year the STRIP is held. This interest is called original issue discount (OID).

The mechanics of stripping a note or bond are as follows. STRIPS can only be created from existing ten-year Treasury notes or thirty-year Treasury bonds. Since these notes or bonds are issued every three months, there is a large eligible pool of issues that can be stripped. Also, any issue that was a ten-year or thirty-year before the program started became eligible. A primary dealer submits a note or bond to the Federal Reserve with certain instructions and the appropriate number of interest coupons, and the corresponding principal is sent back to the primary dealer (in whole numbers only). In the Federal Reserve's mind, they are worth the same amount. To the primary dealer, the note/bond or the STRIPS could be worth more, depending on the demand for a particular side of the trade. Here is what a typical conversion looks like:

> Send two hundred million, 8.875 percent, 2/15/2019 bonds over the Fedwire to the Federal Reserve to be stripped. Receive back from Federal Reserve, over the Fedwire, 8.875 million of every coupon (February and August, from current date to 2/15/2019, which is equal to every interest payment the Federal Reserve needs to make on the 8.875 percent, 2/15/2019 bond) and a two hundred million principal piece, due on 2/15/2019 (the payment of the principal portion is what will be paid out on the bond at maturity). The Federal Reserve is indifferent if they are paying interest on a note/bond or if it has been converted to a STRIP. It is the same amount.

Since each eligible note/bond in the STRIP program has an interest payment schedule based on its coupon/duration and many issues are eligible in the STRIP program, the OID for each STRIP issue is determined by the US Treasury. Today, the STRIPS market is a $200 billion market. The normal bid and ask spread on a treasury issue (bill, note, or bond) is very small. The bid and ask on STRIPS is wider, so investors will not use this product to trade their differing short term interest rate viewpoints; only long term investors will use this product.

My first trade in STRIPS was this. At the time the federal funds rate was about 7 percent. I took it upon myself to do a simple matchbook trade in STRIPS: reversed in thirteen million 11/15/1997 STRIPS (worth about $6 million) at 6 percent from a customer, repo out thirteen million 11/15/1997 STRIPS at 4 percent to a primary dealer; both sides were open. This produced a profit of about $324 per day for Bear Stearns. My customer was happy to make a profit, and the primary dealer was excited to cover a STRIP short. I was happy. The trade was on for thirty-five days, and the total profit equaled $11,340 ($324 * 35). If the repo got returned, I would return the reverse repo. Both had to be done by 10:00 a.m., so there was very little risk. The Bear Stearns traders who solely traded STRIPS had the largest profit-loss book at Bear Stearns in the mid-to-late 1980s. I figured if they could do it in the outright market, there was no reason why I couldn't do it in the repo market. Over the next two to three years, my matchbook in STRIPS swelled to about $125 million in size. Senior Management noticed the profit. Bear Stearns didn't care if you were Irish, black, female, or purple—profit was the most important item.

I had a diverse group of sources from which to borrow STRIPS. They were not your routine accounts, even though they were big, because all dealers looked for STRIPS at the ordinary accounts. Four accounts that stood out to me were the California Public Employees Retirement System (CALPERS), the National Bank of Detroit, First Chicago Bank, and the Connecticut Pension Fund. They were not unusual, but I was often their only STRIP borrower. CALPERS was unique. They would only put out their STRIPS for two-week periods and did it a day forward, unlike the normal same-day cash trade and open. They did not want to be bothered by STRIPS. CALPERS treated their repo in STRIPS like an outright trade. Not many people would want to do this because their short could be covered by the next day. If an issue was very special, I often took the chance. If the trading desk covered their short, although the "typical" position stayed a long time, they were now mine to trade.

In July 1988 I married Caroline. Our first child was born in September 1991. I bought $35,000 8/15/2009 STRIPS to fund her first year of college education.

SIGNATURE TRADE

In about 1991 I developed another STRIPS strategy that would be my signature trade going forward. It started very simply. A dealer who had access to a broker screen (a screen that other dealers could see) had a bid for twenty million 11/15/94 STRIP principals at 4 percent. This bid would go up every day at about 11:00 a.m. and stay there until the end of the day. Effectively, this was a FTD, every day earning 0 percent. I went to all my sources and none had the issue. I was mad and hated seeing that bid every day. How was I going to get the 11/15/94 STRIP principal? I finally figured out how. I would reverse in twenty million of the note, which was the 11.625 percent 11/15/94 (to make it simple, priced at $100). It was the note that by stripping it would create the 11/15/94 principal. After reversing the note, I would send the note to the Federal Reserve to be stripped, receiving the entire STRIP stream back. I would repo the twenty million 11/15/94 principal piece, which was worth about 70 percent of the note or $14 million to the dealer on the broker screen. With the federal funds rate around 6 percent, I reversed in the note at 5.75 percent, I repoed the principal piece at 3 percent and funded the remaining $6 million unsecured with the Bear Stearns Treasury Department at 6.25 percent. I probably could have done a lower rate on the principal, but I wanted the broker to put up more issues. The dealer was very happy that he finally covered his short, and I made a sizeable profit. It was on for about seventy days for a total profit of over $60,000. This was on twenty million of the matchbook balance sheet. The spread was huge.

Unfortunately, I did the first strip as a buy/sell on our books, like the trading desk did. This gave me an outright trading position in every issue created, as well as the associated risk, which I didn't want. I converted them to a standard Finance Desk borrow/pledge transaction (borrow the STRIP stream/pledge the note), which didn't give me outright trading positions but rather finance positions. I had plenty of sources for the note, so I didn't see much of a risk, but there was some. If I got pulled on the note (the person I was borrowing the note from needed it back and I could not borrow the note anyplace else although I could always borrow the issue from the Federal Reserve) and it got very special, I could lower the rate to the borrower on the principal or pull the principal. If I had to pull the principal, it meant I had gotten pulled on the note and it was in demand. I could not just reconstitute the issue (put the note back together), because the principal piece would probably fail to come in, which was the same problem the original borrower had. This would cause me to fail to deliver the note back, costing me more money. I would just reconstitute with the Federal Reserve after I got the twenty-million 11/15/94 principal returned. The net profit was $864 daily which was an approximate 6 to 1 ratio, ($1,040 (profit) / $176 (loss), and my breakeven about six days. (A weekend (three days) would make it 18 days) I think my first day of the trade was a Friday, so I had almost three weeks if everything went wrong until my breakeven. Fortunately, the issue never became scarce.

After my first few experiences, I knew I could expand the trade. STRIPS were not viewed as an exciting or glamourous position on any Finance Desk, so they were often overseen by junior people. I became the best friend to every other Finance Desk's STRIP person. I was often going up against a non–A team player, so my profits were easier but just as real as any other trader. I wanted to have a low profile, so people wouldn't realize how profitable STRIPS could be. I had figured out what to do; now the real trick was how to maximize it. First, since I knew it worked for twenty million, how could I do it for a bigger size? Second, I needed to find the shorts and see what they were asking for. I found out there were many shorts in the marketplace. The original trade was for the principal portion of the STRIPS as opposed to the coupon portion, as these were the majority of the shorts.

As the size of the repo STRIP matchbook grew to about three billion, yes billion, I realized something: reducing cost was a must. I reduced the loss reversing in notes and bonds to less than one basis point, (since the note/bond was undesirable and I was borrowing them on open but for a long time, the lenders lowered the rate drastically) and I reduced the twenty-five-basis-point loss on funding the excess STRIPS to less than two basis points by funding them myself. A new variable also occurred: from all the stripping, I was building a sizeable inventory of coupon STRIPS (forty to fifty million), and I had new demands from the Bear Stearns trading desk to other dealers having coupon shorts. I had become a security lender (which I talked about earlier, page 24); the security lenders were my competition although I didn't have to split my profits with anyone, and I had all the tough issues.

I always let the Bear Stearns trading desk do any stripping or reconstituting they wanted. We were on the same team and it offered them something that no other dealer had. They loved this and took advantage of it whenever they could. The only short for a reconstitution I had to worry about was the principal piece. I had all the coupons (even the hard-to-borrow ones) and usually already had the principal piece. I could cover the trading desk shorts cheaper than our present covering source, saving them money and getting some coupon positions out to other dealers.

In the beginning, all dealers did not have stripping capabilities. I was nimble, on the frontline, and saw the demand. Seeing this demand was made by being in constant contact with all other dealers who were using the product to sell to mainly big accounts. Soon, the STRIP matchbook became very lucrative to Bear Stearns and continued to grow. It consistently added $10 million to $17 million per year to the revenue of Bear Stearns. Some days we made more than others, but from 1991 to 2008 the Finance Desk made over $225 million in STRIP repo revenue without one day of losing money.

I reduced cost by reversing in the notes/bonds from customers at nearly general collateral rates and funded the STRIPS with those same customers in their "investing proceeds area" as opposed to their "lending area". We did both. The lending area loved the consistency I afforded, and they made money by investing in higher-yielding assets. The money we borrowed short term was from an area of the customer that had to invest short-term money. They also loved us. The added bonus was the "netting" given on our balance sheet at quarter ends (netting discussed below but in more detail on page 71).

Since a majority of the borrowing (reverse repos) and funding (repos) was with the same counterparty, even if they didn't know it, much of the STRIP book was "netted," making the return on assets even larger. The profit was the spread on whatever specials I could put out and keep out. The average length of an item put out was about thirty-five days, longer in the beginning and shorter at the end, and the rate rarely changed. Plus, an added benefit occurred: Bear Stearns became very valuable to the customer by reversing in so much, and we now often got the first look at many other special issues, which Tim traded. This was an additional source of revenue to the firm due to the STRIP matchbook.

During the early 1990s, defeasances were plentiful. Defeasances occurred when municipalities had a project and needed a precise cash flow over a specific time period. They often used STRIPS, and the street could not borrow from those accounts. We set up a three-way partnership with the Municipal Department, Treasury Desk, and the Finance Desk—no small feat on Wall Street. The three brought a different set of parameters to the partnership and only one entity had to make a profit as opposed to each area. Municipalities were a constant demand for the STRIPS market. The Municipal Department had two kinds of deals: negotiated, which were for Bear Stearns only, and competitive, which included several dealers, usually five. The negotiated deals were small and few, and over time all deals became competitive. The Municipal Department brought the deal, the Treasury Desk would price the deal, and the Finance Desk would guarantee that all deliveries would be made (usually early, by 11:00 a.m. or 1:00 p.m.) on settlement day. There was an optimization program used to determine the best issues to use in each defeasance. Every dealer had one. We won a few, but there was an added benefit to the Finance Desk even if we lost. I knew which STRIPS were leaving the street. They often became specials.

The other members of the Bear Stearns Finance Desk knew when I had done a very profitable trade because I would rub my hands together quickly. My best trades were a win-win for each party involved. It was very profitable for me, and the customer was happy to have covered his or her short.

I made vice president in 1990, associate director in 1991, managing director in 1992, and, the penultimate, senior managing director (SMD) in 1993. This meteoric rise was tied to profitability.

My second child was born in January 1993. Her college education was funded with STRIPS. At that time I became very conservative about future college costs and bought $65,000 of the STRIP coupon maturing 8/15/11.

RISK

Risk was taken very seriously at Bear Stearns. The risk manager was Mike Winchell. Ace always liked to say, "We may trust you, but we trust you even more when we're watching you." Mike was very good at his job. Every Monday at 4:00 p.m., there would be a risk meeting overseen by Ace and later by Warren Spector (head of fixed income). The manager of every trading desk in the firm attended the meeting. Tim usually went, and occasionally I would go. It was about 20 people, all SMD's. Ace sat in the middle of a long conference table and some people stood. Everyone was in the same spot each week. It was very intimidating. In the same order, each manager would present their revenue for the week, and if someone didn't have a good week, Ace would want to know why. His memory for details was amazing. For example, one event involved a trader from the London office. We were expanding overseas, especially in London. Each week as we grew, the trader would claim his loss was from a firm mistake, not the trader's. After the fourth "mistake," Ace was really mad. He said if they were all honest firm mistakes, some should go our way. That trader did not last long. Eventually, as computer systems became more efficient and allowed senior management to know all the answers beforehand, the weekly meeting was stopped.

No matter how diligent we were at monitoring risk, if someone wanted to steal from us, they could figure out a way. For the most part, individuals didn't come up with a big plan, and they weren't always "bad" people. Usually, the first time they got away with stealing, the theft was small, but then it would snowball. Eventually, they could only get out by getting caught. The firm's goal was not to let it get big or go on for too long.

I saw two cases of someone who tried to beat the firm. I was even closely involved with one. The first happened in the corporate bond department. It was mismarking in thinly traded options. The trader couldn't take his own pressure and told on himself. The second was the head trader of STRIPS on the government desk. For example, from a risk standpoint, the STRIPS trader was long the 11/15/13 coupon and short an equal amount of the 2/15/14 coupon, and although sizeable, it looked fine. He was this way for about ten issues. From a profit-loss viewpoint, it was another story. It represented several million dollars in unrealized gains. These gains would dramatically increase the size of his bonus.

As I said before, the bid and ask on STRIPS was wide—about one-eighth of a point. If we were long an issue, even though we bought at the ask price, our mark was at the bid, or the lower price. If we were short, the mark would be at the ask price. Our unrealized gains and losses should have been based on these prices. But on those issues where we had big positions, the prices were not. The head trader was manipulating the prices, and with substantial positions his discrepancy was large. If other firms knew his positions were very large, the bid and ask on each position would change significantly against him. Since Bear Stearns supplied fixed-income prices to the newspapers, I noticed the problem reading *Barron's* on a Saturday. You could only recognize the pricing problem if you knew the trading positions. On the following Monday, I went through Bear Stearns' positions in detail and showed a few people, including my boss. I was told to watch for one more day. The head trader was found out by the risk department on Monday night. Was it a coincidence? I'm sure the firm wanted the risk group to find an inconsistency, not another trader, but we'll never know.

My saddest workday occurred in the summer of 1994 when I was on the train on my way to work, reading the *Wall Street Journal*. It was the day Joe Jett's deception was discovered at Kidder Peabody. Joe was the head of the trading desk and the STRIP trader. He had figured out a way to beat the internal systems at Kidder Peabody. I think the firm said he had fabricated $300 million in profits. His losses to me were real. I didn't know if they were part of the $300 million or not, and I really didn't care. He did a lot of cash (same-day) stripping. This was very unusual in the STRIP market. It was the last-second decisions that made Kidder always come to Bear Stearns to fill its needs. At the peak, I had $2.7 billion in STRIP specials out to Kidder. The size of the STRIP matchbook was about $9 billion, the largest it would ever be. They were my biggest customer by far and the average spread was approximately thirty basis points. This was worth about $21,000 per day in profit to Bear Stearns. We had even tried to figure out what Kidder was doing. At one point, I asked someone at Bear Stearns, a former rocket scientist, to see if Kidder was doing anything new, but she couldn't figure it out. The advice was to continue what I was doing. I now knew it would all be gone in three months, since they would unwind Joe's entire trading book

Joe Jett was a big contributor to my trade but not the only one. Since I knew I was getting $2.7 billion in STRIPS returned, I had to find another way to trade those STRIPS, but how? I had to learn how to manage the book better. I did shrink the book to about $6 billion but figured out some new ways to replace Joe's income.

Two new ways to trade the book were very straightforward, and the other was more creative. The first way was to sell the short Treasury STRIP coupons in the outright market. I had created them when I'd reversed in issues and stripped them. By this time, I had amassed an inventory of about 130 million of every February and August STRIP coupons and about 110 million of every May and November STRIP coupons. I would watch the short outright STRIP market, which was unheard of by a repo STRIP trader. If there were at least thirty basis points between selling the short STRIP and reversing an equal amount of an issue in on term repo. I would sell the STRIP. I converted some of the open reverse repos to term dates to match the size and maturing date of the STRIP I sold. (Remember, the notes/bonds were reversed in on open with the rate negotiated each day to match the interest rate on the repo STRIP funding; as it turned out, some open trades were on for over ten years. Since the STRIP funding was now on term, I made the reverse of the note/bond to the same date offsetting the risk.) This would accomplish two items: the spread from the sale and the reverse repo would be "locked in" for a long period and my interest rate risk exposure would not change even though I did a longer trade (both sides had the same date). Always mindful of my own risk, I limited myself to selling 75 percent of my three-month STRIP position, 50 percent of the six-month STRIP position, and 25 percent of the nine-month and one-year STRIP positions. With every passing day, the minimal risk (from selling the STRIP) got even smaller as the maturity got closer. Since the price was very high, the profitability locked in was substantial and essentially risk free. I wish I had thought of it sooner. Thank you, Joe.

The second way was actually doing my trade but in reverse. I reconstituted a shorter issue. The issue had to be trading special. This was made easier by our seating arrangement. I backed up to Tim and Kevin Shannon, our government specials traders. If I could find the principal piece, reconstitute the issue, and give it to them to trade, Bear Stearns would be a winner in two ways. This was extremely profitable for the STRIP matchbook, because the whole issue was priced around $100 (at a low interest rate) and the principal piece, the only piece I had to borrow, was not. I can't remember how many I did, but the largest reconstitution was about three hundred million. Plus, since we were usually short, it would really take pressure off an issue if a new, sizeable supply was hitting the market, and the Bear Stearns specials traders knew it.

The third way was harder and more creative. If I had an issue all out to many people on repo, knew it was very hard to find, and the likelihood of delivery back to me was very remote, I would pull (call back) the issue, even though I didn't need to (usually on a Friday). In most instances, but not all, it would create a significant FTR. As a reminder, this was extremely profitable, and a FTR was like a repo at 0 percent. This had a risk to it. I couldn't do it very often or the other person might not borrow from me in the first place or wouldn't use me as their first call, thereby eliminating my chance to ever use this option.

I had a unique relationship with the team of people who worked at Drexel Burnham (later other primary dealers) headed by Mike. He was a big short in the market. Mike and his team covered the trading position and had a small, profitable matchbook in STRIPS. He covered everything he could away from me and only came to me at the last minute or for a very special issue. He was the other A player in STRIPS. He didn't know exactly what I was doing, but he knew I was profitable. Since he was a big player, he knew STRIPS were a valuable product.

REWARDS

After his 1986 to 1994 term as a Governor at the Federal Reserve, Wayne Angell was hired by Bear Stearns as chief economist. This was a major coup for Bear Stearns. He helped the Finance Desk with his early interest rate predictions.

Bear Stearns was run by the executive committee. These were the top people in the firm. In the early 1990s, it was made up of nine people. My boss, Vinny Mattone, was one of them. One would think as the firm got larger and expanded into more products, this committee would grow. It did the exact opposite; it shrank. In the 2000s there were only five people on the committee. Power was king, and the people who had power were not going to share it. Part of the sizeable compensation packages awarded to this group should have been plowed back into the company. The top management of our small investment bank wanted to be paid like the biggest; they wanted to show they were as important. It really made a difference at the end.

Our year-end changed several times during my tenure at Bear Stearns, from April 30 to June 30 and then November 30. The first date was awkward for analysts. The second was better for the analysts, but since our second quarter ended on December 31, like banks' year-ends, we could not take advantage of it. The third date was OK for analysts, and we were off cycle from the banks. Since this last change took seventeen months, Bear Stearns' employees were given some stock that vested over three years for staying around. Most stayed around.

The Bear Stearns CAP (Capital Accumulation Plan) plan required all senior employees to be owners of company stock. It was locked up for five years. Every year, the stock would earn interest and grow (like dividends, but supercharged). This wasn't unique to Bear Stearns, although we had to defer more than others, and it was very profitable because the stock kept rising. Fortunately, I sold every share after the required five-year holding period, hoping it was a bad sale. I still had five years of stock I couldn't touch that I hoped would make more money in the future. Also, from a risk standpoint, I didn't want all my assets tied to one entity. At my peak I had about 46 percent of my assets tied up in Bear Stearns stock; at the end it was about the lowest but still a sizeable 22 percent. Unfortunately, others were not as fortunate, as I found out in 2008. Many senior people, feeling Bear Stearns was a safe investment, just sold enough to pay taxes and put the CAP stock into their individual account. This decision proved disastrous.

In the early 1990s, Bear Stearns started a 401(k) plan. I always contributed the maximum. Bear Stearns would always grant stock to an employee stock plan (ESOP) for anyone less than an SMD. It was based on tenure. There was a bonus paid every year. Bear Stearns had two types of bonuses. The first would depend solely on how profitable a year it was for Bear Stearns. For the people who were paid bi-weekly on the clock (how I was originally paid in the training program) their bonus would consist of several weeks' pay (usually 2-14). A salaried employee would collect the major portion of his/her yearly compensation in the bonus (possibly several times the annual salary, mostly dependent on the individual's contribution to the firm. If an employee was not happy with his/her bonus, they might leave but Bear Stearns was comprised of long term employees, leaving was rare.) For SMDs a major portion of their compensation was in stock. The Finance Desk was special. We had two distinct functions. We brought in revenue to the firm and provided a funding service to many other departments.

No matter the cash amount of my bonus, each year I used it the same way: 10 percent immediately for some fun thing, 10-20 percent for college for the kids, and 70-80 percent to either pay down debt or invest for the future. I would buy a variety of fixed-income bonds and stock in large, well-known companies that paid decent dividends. This would prove fruitful in my later years. Also, I would always buy some stock in the companies where my friends worked. It didn't matter how much. It always gave me something to talk about with them, and it was usually a good investment.

It seemed like I was always getting paid at different times of the year. The CAP disbursement would come right after year-end. I always participated in the forward-sale process offered by Bear Stearns; this allowed each participant to sell his or her maturing five-year position over a three-month period. Again, from a risk standpoint, I sold my amount over about sixty business days, or about three months. My feeling was if I held stock for five years, why wouldn't I want to spread out the sale of my position? The other two alternatives were to sell all my stock on one day or sell enough to cover my taxes on that one day and put the remaining shares in my account. The major buyer of the Bear Stearns stock was that year's CAP plan. That one day always showed a huge volume. I sold the earnings for that year in February because that was when they were disbursed.

The stock that was given to employees when our year-end changed from June to November vested in June, so I would sell it at that point. My bonus came after our year-end, although that changed over time from two weeks to two months. This happened for two reasons: the firm earned interest on the money for a longer period of time, and doing this would stop people from leaving because they were already two months into the following year bonus cycle. For the most part, people would only leave after they got paid their bonus, so at least Bear Stearns got two months of production from them if they left.

One very good year for me was 1995. Vinny left in a power struggle and I was appointed co-head of the Bear Stearns Finance Desk with my good friend, Tim Greene. Never before had a STRIP trader run a desk. I think being innovative, motivated and profitable were the major reasons I was chosen. I kept a low profile. That is what made the STRIP matchbook so successful. I'm sure a few competitors couldn't figure out why I was appointed.

My third daughter was born in July 1995, and her years in college would be funded by STRIPS.

CHARITY

Charitable giving was very important at Bear Stearns. The company had a mandatory 4 percent charitable rule. Each SMD had to donate 4 percent of his or her gross income to charities of his or her choice. Since compensation was about half of revenue, the 4% was tens of millions of dollars each year. We made a lot and were expected to give back to society. I wasn't sure why other firms didn't require it from senior management, but Bear Stearns was the only one to my knowledge who did. By making it mandatory, it instilled a charitable value into every SMD.

From 1993 to 2008 I adhered to the 4% rule. During the first few years I was a SMD, I had to submit my tax returns to the firm to make sure I complied. In later years a letter from my accountant that stated I'd met the 4 percent threshold sufficed. In the beginning I didn't have a particular charity that I wanted to donate to, so I opened a Fidelity Charitable gift fund account, into which I put money. It counted as my yearly charitable contribution, but I was in control of granting the money. In addition, my contribution grew over time because it was invested in mutual funds. At a later date, I was able to contribute a significant sum to a charity of my choice. I still use it today.

Vinny was very generous. Each time a fellow SMD asked for a donation to a cause (it didn't matter what), he would write a substantial check. Later on, Vinny became very involved with Archbishop Renato Martino and the Holy See mission. This was the Vatican mission to the United Nations. He tried to raise money for his cause. Many at Bear Stearns whom Vinny generously supported turned a blind eye and suddenly became forgetful. I donated a big check. He never forgot.

Christmas was always a special day around the Marren household. When we were kids, we would go to bed on Christmas Eve, and there would be nothing; when we awoke the next morning, Santa had come to our house, and everything was magically transformed. A fully decorated tree appeared in our living room, with wrapped presents spilling out from underneath. It was everything a child could imagine. As a parent later on, I marveled at how my parents did it. The first Christmas after I began working, I gave my mother a trip to London. It was fun planning her trip. On two subsequent Christmases, she went to Paris and Rome. I knew then what it was like to surprise someone. It is truly better to give than to receive.

Bear Stearns always had a Christmas party for the employees' children. Santa Claus was played by fellow SMD's Tom Meade or Andrew Taddei. When my children were young, they looked forward to a day at daddy's office each year. Santa would present each child with a wrapped gift. It was followed by a magic show by the resident magician, Ace Greenberg.

THE LATER YEARS

LEADERSHIP RESPONSIBILITIES

During the 1980s I was told about two penny stocks that were sure bets: Dermalock and Qsound. I learned there was no such thing as a sure bet. People on the Finance Desk lost most of their small investment, myself included. Qsound became known as "Quick Sand." Becoming a senior managing director offered the same challenges; being one did not mean life from then on was a "sure bet."

In the late 90's, the 4:00 p.m. Monday meeting had a new twist. Each department usually reported revenue of between $1 million and $10 million per week, until the mortgage department, which was made up of many groups, began to report consistent revenues of over $20 million per week, and sometimes a lot more. This was staggering to everyone in the room.

There was a big shakeup in the top ranks in 1995, Vinny left and Tim and I were made co-heads of the desk. Warren was put solely in charge of all fixed-income departments. This was partly based on his merits in the mortgage department as well as attrition in the top fixed-income ranks. As head of all fixed income, not just head of mortgages, he could not have every department report directly to him (there were too many to be efficient), so we got to choose who we reported to. We picked Wendy de Moncheaux, the head of derivatives, who reported directly to Warren (Paul Friedman later became our boss, although Wendy always stayed involved.) From a risk viewpoint, she would bring a new and different perspective to the Finance Desk. Also, Wendy had so much already on her plate, and she had confidence in Tim and me, so we hoped she would leave us alone. Wendy did bring a new concept to the desk: value at risk (VAR). VAR measured our forward risk. She was extremely risk conscious and her VAR system was implemented. Since the Finance Desk didn't take a lot of risk, we thought we would be fine, and we were, since most of our trades were overnight.

Tim Greene was very smart. He graduated from West Point, but more importantly, he didn't forget a thing. This was truly a blessing as a trader but also a curse. If you ever did anything to cross him, he would never forget it. After the big change and we took control, we showed that the Finance Desk was harder than it looked: we lost $6 million. From a department that always made a profit to register a loss like this was very unusual. One of Tim's trading strategies sounded very simple. When he saw an opportunity, he shorted a current on-the-run issue to the next refunding date (three months or less away) and fought the daily fight to cover his short. Over time he got very good at this and made much more money than he lost. This was not that time. We immediately marched into Warren's office and informed him of the trading problem, discovered in part by using Wendy's VAR system. Warren could cut to the heart of a problem faster than anyone I ever knew. He asked Tim a lot of questions, but the one question I remember was "If you had to do it all again, given the same set of facts, would you do anything different?" Tim's answer was simply, "I would do it exactly the same." To this day, Tim feels there was some very unusual activity on the issue. Warren was not happy, but had more respect for the Finance Desk and our decision making.

The repo desk accounting method was cash. This meant that as revenue was realized, it was recorded. Through the concept of VAR, we marked all our forward trades. We always knew our forward gains or losses, but did not report them. Our trading income was realized daily.

Other departments' accounting methods were accrual, which meant every position was marked, and we could earn or lose money even if a position had not been sold. For the most part, positions did not last very long. As Warren Spector put it succinctly, "We are moving men, not holders of inventory."

Since the banking system could not be closed four straight days, it was always open the day after Thanksgiving. We would let our Finance Desk team work it out so some would have that Friday off. The people who worked that day would get the day before Christmas or the day after off. This was not counted as a vacation day.

As I rose in title in the firm, I got more vacation time. As an SMD I was entitled to five weeks. Tim and I didn't even know this until the early 2000s. Our policy was if someone needed time off, he or she should take it. Trading was a hard business. Tim and I needed people at their best. People wouldn't abuse this because their bonus was mostly based on what they earned. At commercial banks, every senior employee was required to take four weeks off and at least two straight weeks each year to make sure he or she was not doing anything fraudulent. I thought this was a good policy and investment banks should have adopted it.

Tim and I always talked about the best way to build our franchise. Three of the many things that Tim and I did were: have an annual party for our support staff, try to hire from the operations training program, and get paid the same salary and bonus. The support staff admired the Finance Desk and wanted to do anything they could to help us. They would always put any job of ours at the top of their pile, not just because of the annual party, but because we appreciated their hard work. No other department did this. The individuals on the Finance Desk were all smart and hungry. Many came up from the operations training program, where Tim and I began our career. We were always in the trenches with our team, unlike most other dealers, whose leaders didn't involve themselves with the daily functions. We dealt with the managerial aspects after trading hours. The loyalty and team strength we built up from the people who worked for us was extraordinary. We were more than a well-functioning unit; we were more like an extended family. Whether Tim's trading produced more profits or I did, we always got paid the same amount. There was never any competition between us. It was very unusual for the dog-eat-dog Wall Street mentality.

Before Bear Stearns moved into our own building at 383 Madison Avenue in 2002, we were nearby at 245 Park Avenue. As the building was nearing completion, Tim and I decided to take a tour. We went over at lunchtime. Since there were seven hundred construction workers and only two outside elevators, they took us to the top, dropped us off, and told us to walk down. The building had forty-nine floors, and many were double floors. It was over eight hundred feet tall. Tim and I walked down and looked at our area on the seventh floor. It was state of the art. The next day our legs hurt a lot. The other thing I remember from 383 Madison Avenue was the direct connection to the Metro North train. I never had to go outside to get to and from work.

383 Madison Avenue was the crown jewel of Jimmy Cayne's time as CEO. It was majestic and state of the art. During our last few years at 245 Park Avenue, we spent little money on capital improvements, but everything at 383 Madison was brand new. It had a gym, which was a luxury that became vital for me later on. Tim and I even had an office, though we rarely used it.

Each year we did use our office to meet with our employees and give them their respective bonus. I would make a similar pitch every year. Each person's total compensation was determined in this way:

1. How the person performed
2. How the Finance Desk did as a whole
3. How the fixed-income floor performed
4. How the firm performed

I also reminded our employees that one year didn't make their career. Vinny had been especially good at this. He always knew the smallest amount to pay a person that was just enough to make him or her come back and be hungrier than ever the following year. For Tim and me, with the Finance Desk's profits rising every year, the yearly compensation of each individual was higher without exception.

KEEPING UP APPEARANCES

Quarter-ends were very big around Wall Street. How could a firm shrink its balance sheet to look the best in the analysts' eyes? Since the Finance Desk was short term, it was the ideal place to shrink. On those four occasions (February 28, May 31, August 31, and November 30), we would reduce our portion of the firm's balance sheet. One way was to return our least valuable borrows; this would reduce the asset size. But the biggest impact was to maximize our netting. By reducing our balance sheet size, we improved our return on assets (ROA). By having a better ROA than our peers, theoretically, our stock was more valuable, and management had used its assets more efficiently. The concept of netting a repo and a reverse repo by accounting standards was seen as a reduction of risk, thereby decreasing our total assets. This was viewed favorably. Our ROA was drastically improved. The analysts wanted to see how efficient we were, but they knew every firm did some window dressing, although they never knew how much.

Bear Stearns did it this way. On the Finance Desk, how we wrote the tickets was important. By accounting standards several rules had to be met, but the main two were having the same counterparty and the same end date. In reality, open trades were the same as overnight trades, since either party could close them out; however, accountants didn't see it that way. Internal costs were different as well, since overnight trades were written every day, but open trades were not.

At quarter-ends, we didn't care about ticket costs. During the early days, we matched our Treasury trades with the same counterparty and wrote those trades overnight, thereby netting with that customer. We also made sure any open transaction was written as overnight. After the advent of Government Securities Clearing Corporation (GSCC) previous day repo/reverse repo and outright trades were netted nightly by GSCC, and our same-day repo and reverse-repo trades were converted to GSCC after fifteen minutes. All dealers were participants in the GSCC. This was a brilliant strategy because it reduced counterparty risk and drastically reduced deliveries. In addition, it actually allowed dealers to net more easily, since all counterparties were now GSCC. Since they netted more in their daily activities, all dealers were able to increase their balance sheets.

In later years we would use GSCC to fund our entire general collateral business, mortgage and treasury repos. Since Bear Stearns was usually short Treasury current issues, we borrowed everything in GSCC. Since both sides met the accounting criteria, they netted. At the end we were netting 40-50 percent of the Finance Desk balance sheet on those four days. The cost was relatively minimal but operationally intense. It took about five days to set up, with the last day (reporting day) being the most stressful. It took one day to put it back on. We wanted to use our customer base daily and not GSCC although the netting accomplished our goal of shrinking. At the time, every bank did it to some extent; some shrank more than others.

By having our year-end on November 30, we were able to take advantage of the mandatory commercial bank year-end on December 31, as well as all their quarters. December 31 was a different day. Banks wanted their books to look pristine. Some of our general collateral trades were pegged to the opening federal funds rate. It was always higher than usual. We always wanted to be finished early, because all senior people left early or weren't even there for New Year's Eve. We never wanted a problem on that day.

MAXIMIZING PROFITS

After being appointed co-head of the Finance Desk, I knew there were two ways to increase profits: increase revenues or decrease expenses. I dove into the second one. I found a lot of waste. There were several things but three stood out. The first was the enormous pile of reports we got every day. We could now get them online or eliminate them altogether. The second one was startling. As risk was paramount at Bear Stearns, a former associate had put in a dedicated phone line to his house to make sure Bear Stearns was always safe. He had left two years previously. Bear Stearns was still paying $131 per month for that line. It was cancelled. Another major component of Wall Street was direct phone lines to customers. We had about 10. Some were paid by the customer, some were paid by Bear Stearns, and others were split. An outside line was relatively inexpensive; a direct line was $500 to $900 per month. Needless to say, we dramatically reduced our direct lines. If we had to have one, the other party paid. If it was us, we called them on the less expensive outside line.

While I focused on expenses, Tim focused on increasing revenues; he had an analogy to football, "block and tackle." This simply meant do the basic things really well, and the entire desk did. We led by example.

It made a difference in people's attitude and the profitability of the desk.

Over the years, as we became more technologically advanced, many people lost manual capabilities. When the computer went down, the younger people on the desk would just sit and wait until the computer came back up. The Finance Desk did not wait. It closed every day. Tim and I would revert to manual, and the rest of the Finance Desk learned how to do it. It saved us a few times!

Even though most years blend together, issues and events do not. The 11/15/96 STRIP coupon was a beast. They became very special. I think they were all locked away in defeasances. You could not borrow them. I used that opportunity to pull mine all back. Over one hundred million failed to come in for almost one year. This was very beneficial to Bear Stearns. On that issue alone, the profit was huge (about $4 million).

The other item I remember distinctly was the 1996 Sunday winter snowstorm. During the winter months, if snow was forecast, the various Finance Desks would have their most important traders put up in hotels nearby to make sure their A team met the call the following morning. Since the storm was on a Sunday, other Finance Desks didn't have their A teams that Monday. However, I called everyone at home on Sunday and had them get to a hotel in New York City. We had our A team. We were up against other dealers' D teams, or in some instances, no one at all. Just being there meant the difference. It was a very profitable day at Bear Stearns.

As the STRIP book grew in size (seven billion was the average), it was more about managing it as opposed to single trades. Individual trades came and went. I always wanted to put out as many specials as possible, but it was the overall spread in the book that mattered. We had a report that monitored the overall spread in each matchbook. The STRIP matchbook rarely went below ten basis points and was mostly in the range of fifteen to twenty basis points and sometimes significantly higher. In the beginning the number of A traders in STRIPS were Mike and me, now there were many more as other dealers figured out STRIPS could be profitable. It was harder to make money and get specials out.

Since the primary focus of the Finance Desk was to fund the firm, anytime the Finance Desk matchbook and the firm trading accounts were on different sides of a trade (one was long and the other short or vice versa) Bear Stearns intercompany trades were done. These were done to minimize trades to the outside world. It was always done at an average rate. Both sides would get the best that the Finance Desk could do. After a while this was switched to the 10:00 a.m. broker average to provide a bigger sample.

Bear Stearns had a large captured customer. We did all their funding. It was known as the 10/11 office. The markup was fifty basis points when I started and fifteen basis points when it all ended. It was a good deal for both parties. For Bear Stearns, it was a consistent source of revenue ($5 million at the beginning and $2 million at the end). For the customer, it was a constant and reliable source of funding.

Our last child was born in 1998. His college tuition was funded by STRIPS, just like his siblings.

ATMOSPHERE

Bear Stearns had great benefits. Similar to the 4 percent charity rule, if you made more, you paid more for the same benefits than a lesser-paid employee. With benefit costs always rising, Bear Stearns was attempting to be fair to all its employees.

Bear Stearns had a nepotism policy; we couldn't hire a family member or relative of a current employee. Ace said, "I'm sure we lost a few good people over the years, but we also saved Bear Stearns from some disasters."

Bear Stearns often hired well-known people in sales or would take a risk on a person: Richard Todd (quarterback for the Jets), Steve Janaszak (backup goalie on the 1980 US Olympic hockey team), Gerard Phelan (a Boston College graduate who caught the Hail Mary pass from Doug Flutie), Don Maloney (played for the New York Rangers), as well as other sports figures. Additionally, well-respected individuals from outside the sports world were hired, including former New York Governor Hugh Carey and former Federal Reserve Governor Wayne Angell. I'm sure there were more. They used their fame to get in and since they knew a lot of people usually did fine.

On one occasion the head specials trader wasn't feeling well. The stress of the job and being overweight had given him a mild heart attack.

Since he was heavy, Tim and I gave the paramedics a hand down to the ambulance. Both Tim and I thought we had to lift him into the ambulance. Because of the way a stretcher works, the legs folded up, and he slid right in. Tim and I got a surprise by not having to lift him into the ambulance. Fortunately, he recovered quickly and was back at work.

Every first Monday of the month, there was an SMD meeting. It was held in a big conference room. It was overseen by Ace Greenberg and then Jimmy Cayne. They would tell of the most recent accomplishments by the firm. When I first made SMD, each newly minted SMD was required to give a speech about what he or she did. It was not a pleasant experience, especially if a person didn't talk in front of others often. I remember talking in generalities, and my speech went fine. The speeches were stopped after a few years, but the SMD meeting carried on until the end.

There was a big SMD event each year. These were stopped after my first two years for two reasons: to reduce costs and because there were too many SMDs. It was a tradition from the partner days when there were far fewer people. These events were held at the Pierre Hotel and a fellow SMD's house. They were lavish.

Almost every year after I made SMD, it was suggested that I make a contribution to the Bear Stearns political action committee (PAC). It was always for $500, and I always contributed. During the 2008 presidential race, candidates from both parties gave presentations to SMDs in the Bear Stearns conference room. It was very enlightening to see them up close.

GIVING

Employees at Bear Stearns including myself supported a lot of charity events. In 1998 Jaime Held joined us from the Derivative Department. Jaime was smart and a very likeable guy. He knew the spread on all currencies and the sports scores from the night before. He was the perfect addition to the Finance Desk. Unfortunately at the young age of 39, Jaime passed away from a brain tumor.

After his passing, we discovered Jaime's special friendship with Ed Lucas. Ed was affiliated with the New Jersey School for the Blind. Jaime and Ed had met at a baseball game, and they'd both shared a love for the New York Yankees. Ed was associated with a golf event run by Phil Rizzuto. In 2001, Tim and I became lead sponsors of the event. At the event I was paired in the same golf cart as Yogi Berra. We got to the first hole, and the group proceeded to hit four balls out of bounds. Yogi said Bob Feller's (Hall of Fame pitcher) group would tee it right up again, so we did. At the dinner that night, there was an enormous amount of Yankees memorabilia, including over one hundred signed baseballs. I wanted to get something for my son, Peter. There was a Paul O'Neill bat in the silent auction that would be perfect. I bid on the bat, but there was someone else who was interested. Since I didn't know if I won and I had to go home with something, I turned to the live auction. There were two signed bats being auctioned off. They were combined, and I was the highest bidder. As it worked out, I came home with three bats. One is a signed Derek Jeter Rookie of the Year bat. It is my son's prize possession.

My last boss, Paul Friedman, was very involved with the charity Cancer Care. For years he would take me to the Connecticut chapter event and he would take Tim to the Long Island chapter event. It was always fun and opened me up to a future opportunity.

For Tim's fiftieth birthday, I wanted to do something unique. At the Cancer Care event in Connecticut, I purchased a three-day golf event in Monterey, California, given by Lexus Champions for Charity. Lexus Champions for Charity gave to a variety of charities around the country. They gave each charity the opportunity to have a twosome participate in their golf tournament in California. It was a blast, and it brought Tim back to his old stomping grounds when he was in the army and stationed at Fort Ord, California. Tim would often remind me that nobody ever attacked the West Coast when he was there. We had fun at the golf event with about two hundred other twosomes from around the country. We played at Pebble Beach, Spanish Bay, and Spyglass. The top twenty-five groups won money for their charity. We didn't play well, and our goal was to make it off the last page of scores. We never did.

NEW PRODUCTS

Around 2003 a new product on the mortgage side was called whole-loan funding. It was overseen by Gerald McCrink. Gerald was smart, had an accounting background, and was very conservative. Tim and I felt very confident in him. Although we were small in this product, the spreads were enticing. To be even more profitable, Wall Street wanted the suppliers of the loans. Morgan Stanley paid $706 million for the mortgage originator, Saxon, in August 2006. Merrill Lynch bought a mortgage originator, First Franklin Financial, for $1.3 billion in September 2006. But Bear Stearns paid just $27 million that Fall for their originator, Encore Credit Corporation. Bear Stearns would never overpay. As my parents told me and almost everyone knew, "If something sounds too good to be true, it usually is."

The concept of tri-party repo was a win-win-win for dealers, customers, and clearing banks. Although the concept of tri-party repo started earlier it really got big in the late 1990's. Tri-party repo was not delivering general collateral over the Fedwire or having the collateral returned the following day. The customer would send his or her money to the clearing bank, the dealer would assign a certain type of collateral to that money, (all their collateral was at the clearing bank) and then the clearing bank would release the funds to the dealer, collecting a small fee. This dramatically cut down the activity on the Fedwire as well as the cost to the dealer to fund smaller positions. Bear Stearns did several billion dollars per day in the beginning and built up to about $15 billion per day at the end. Also, it was a good way for dealers to check prices. We looked at any bank prices that were 1 percent different from ours. Since many of the securities were complex, it was re-assuring to us to have an independent pricing source. With the cost of tri-party so low, it allowed dealers to have bigger balance sheets.

A potentially thorny issue turned into a fortuitous one. Shauna Richman was our mortgage matchbook trader. She was great at her job—very good with customers and very knowledgeable about the mortgage product. She and I graduated from college the same year— she from Lehigh University and I from Bucknell University. Shauna was expecting a baby. It was difficult losing our head mortgage trader for three months, but we managed. As a father, I know how difficult parenting can be, especially the first time. I can't imagine how hard it is to be a mother, never mind a mother with a job. Of course, this was not just any job but an exceptionally stressful one as well. Shortly after Shauna's first child was born she became pregnant again. Tim and I had a difficult decision. We couldn't lose our head mortgage match-book trader for another three months, and we couldn't lose Shauna. We moved a young, very talented person into the head mortgage match-book position, and we created a new job for Shauna upon her return: she was the sole person in charge of fixed-income prime brokerage, re-porting to Tim and me. After a short time (and given Shauna's talents), this business took off. In a few years, it was a five-member team, and we were the envy of Wall Street. It consistently made a profit. It was one of the businesses that JPMorgan Chase wanted from the Finance Desk after the merger. The team is still there, with Shauna leading it.

FOREIGN OFFICES

Twice a year Tim or I went to London and in later years stopped at our small office in Dublin as well. One trip I took was particularly memorable, but not for business reasons. I packed my bag at home but felt I was forgetting something. When I checked in, I realized I had forgotten my passport. I called home, and Caroline found it. She loaded the four kids in the minivan and drove to the airport. I made the flight.

Liquid Funding Limited (LFL) was our subsidiary based in Dublin, Ireland. It was situated there to take advantage of Ireland's low corporate tax rate. LFL was created by our derivative department and was an off-balance-sheet funding solution that gave us the opportunity for additional leverage. This special-purpose vehicle (SPV) was a trust, and because of the diversity and quality of the collateral, it was given AAA status by the rating agencies. LFL was funded by commercial paper issued by the trust, and because of the AAA rating, it was very cheap. The Finance Desk made approximately $5 million annually.

It was very comforting to Tim and me to have Jon Ferber in our London office. Jon had worked with us in New York and was very much like us. Jon would make decisions similar to Tim and me, allowing us to sleep comfortably every night. As the office expanded, Jon added a few people. One was John Paul, who was six feet two and weighed 260 pounds. He was a black belt in karate and could still do a split. No one ever believed he could do it, but he won a few bets in the London pubs by proving he could.

CHANGES

In the early 2000s, Tim got married. I wanted to do something special for him. We ended up going to Las Vegas for his bachelor party. It was during the Sweet Sixteen weekend of March Madness NCAA basketball. At Tim's request we made golf tee times for early Saturday morning. We woke to a sunny but blustery day. Tim didn't want to play. I said fine, but seven of us went anyway. When we arrived at Bali Hai, they were offering refunds to anyone who didn't want to play because of the wind. I said it was too windy for one person (Tim).

There were different trading functions on the Finance Desk. In my early days, the only large profit-and-loss areas on the Finance Desk were Treasury specials, on and off the run, and the 10/11 office. It now consisted of seven main areas: Treasury matchbook, STRIP matchbook, prime brokerage, LFL, London business, Mortgage matchbook, and a few smaller ones. The Treasury matchbook and Mortgage matchbook consisted of several products. We had grown diverse over the years and now consistently made $100 million in revenue per annum, as well as executing our main function, which was funding the firm. Although Vinny had passed away a few years prior, he would have been proud.

The number of primary dealers over the years shrank dramatically, from about forty when I started to about twenty at the end. A primary dealer was a bank or securities broker/dealer who was permitted to trade directly with the Federal Reserve. Firms were required to make bids or offers when the Federal Reserve conducted open-market operations, provide information to the Federal Reserve open-market trading desk, and participate actively in US Treasury security auctions. Many former employees of primary dealers worked at the Treasury because of their expertise in the government debt markets. Shrinkage was due to one main factor: mergers. Being a primary dealer was demanding, given all the requirements, but it was also very important.

The demise of Long-Term Capital Management (LTCM) occurred in 1998. We cleared for LTCM; they used us as a processor for all their trades. Even though LTCM lost a lot of money, Bear Stearns didn't lose a penny. Tim always made sure Bear Stearns was safe and secure. Clearing for them was enough risk for the firm.

SPORTS CULTURE

Sports knowledge and small wagers were a very big part of our desk. Tim's family had season tickets to the Giants for over fifty years, and Tim was a huge fan of West Point football. Sports were a good way to build camaraderie on our desk and a great way to stimulate communication among traders. There always seemed to be box pools for the Super Bowl, major golf tournaments, and even betting on the Triple Crown. There were three good stories associated with office pools. One was about NCAA March Madness, the second was about horse racing, and the last, which continues today, was about the NFL pool.

The NCAA pool was a Sweet Sixteen bet. We picked the names out of a hat. Tim and I had two picks but were partners in each pick. His pick lost, and mine was Kentucky. In the final four, Warren Spector wanted to pay for a piece of Kentucky. I gladly let him purchase a piece, especially since he decided our bonuses. Kentucky won. Tim thought I gave it away.

The second story is even better. I was away for two horse-racing pools and managed to win both. The day before the Kentucky Derby I was out of the office so Tim put in my money for the pool, On Monday, I was handed $190 for picking Barbaro. Two weeks later I was out again. Tim made the call that everyone on the Finance Desk would go in together and we would "box the triple" for the Preakness, but we couldn't pick the favorite, Barbaro. Barbaro broke his leg, and that Monday I was handed $700. I joked that I should take more days off.

The third story concerns a bet but also a forced get-together. I first entered the NFL pool early in my Finance Desk career. The wager was an NFL season-long bet. It was against the spread, and there were five games picked each week. One was the Jets, one was the Giants, and then three other NFL games. At the end of the year, the bottom half of the participants took the top half out. Going out meant, hors d'oeuvres and cocktails at Harry's on Hanover Square, dinner at a swanky steak restaurant, cocktails after, cab rides home, breakfast the following morning, and shoe shines. The group consisted of twelve to sixteen people. I lost my first year, and it cost me $425, almost as much as my two-week take home pay. I have won more times than I have lost. The picks and get together are alive today with former Bear Stearns colleagues.

In 1993 the Finance Desk purchased Yankees season tickets. There are two memorable Yankees stories. The first one happened during the 2005 season. Since the Finance Desk had been season ticket holders for a long time, we knew the people around us. We swapped our seats for one game. We gave up our four seats to a Red Sox game in exchange for four seats to a Seattle Mariners game. The other people couldn't believe their luck, and we were able to bring our Japanese customers to see Ichiro. John Ryding, Bear Stearns' chief economist, went with the group. It surely helped bring in new repo business. The second story involves tickets to the World Series. Jack Chimento, Marc Toscano, Tim, and I were going to the game. (Jack and Marc were vital parts to the Bear Stearns fixed income business) After a great dinner, we headed up to the stadium by subway. I had given everyone a ticket, but my ticket was stolen by a pickpocket on the subway. I eventually got in after the ticket taker verified that I was the ticket holder. The person who'd bought my stolen ticket showed up in the third inning. He had paid $1,000 for the ticket. He understood it was my seat and realized he would be unable to sit down but was still happy to be in the stadium and witnessing the game. The Yankees won.

In 1999 Caroline and I bought a cottage in Chatham on Cape Cod. In 2000 we renovated it and have spent many summers there. It was also a very timely investment. I sunk the majority of my bonus during those two years into the cottage instead of into the stock market, which was in a free fall due to the dot-com bust. Our niece dubbed it later, "the greatest Yankees house in Red Sox nation."

I loved to coach youth basketball in my hometown of Darien. I coached my two older daughters when they were young and before "Travel Hoops" in fifth grade for Meg. It was a great way to meet their friends. There was a practice on a weekday night and a game each Saturday from December until February, followed by playoffs. The most important thing for the girls to learn was to have fun playing basketball. Borrowing a page from Tim's block and tackle basic skills, I made the girls become proficient at dribbling and layups. We won a lot of games. Later, because of my health, I only coached Peter for a year.

Every May since graduation, a group of mostly college fraternity brothers (FIJI) and I have gone to Hilton Head Island to play golf. Tim joined us one year. The Red Stackloaf Golf Classic became the name of this weekend getaway. I had been going to Hilton Head since childhood, and it was the ideal place to reconnect every year. I was the planner. There were between eight and twenty guys every year. Many of the hours spent preparing for this event occurred after work hours at Bear Stearns. The Red Stackloaf Golf Classic is now in its thirty-second consecutive year.

Over the years I have played many golf courses. One of the perks of my job was the ability to play courses not ordinarily available to non-members. Most were corporate outings, some were Bear Stearns entertainment, and some were charity outings. Three stories stand out.

The first happened at Pebble Beach. I flew out to see a customer and to play Spanish Bay the next day with him. I arrived a day early to play the mecca of golf, Pebble Beach. It was about one-thirty in the afternoon when I got there, and I asked the starter if I could go out as soon as possible. He said he would see what he could do. At three o'clock, I was still waiting. I returned to the starter, gave him one hundred dollars, and somehow I was in the next group. While on a subsequent trip to visit the same customer and play golf at Spanish Bay, another invitee had an unfortunate mix-up. The closest airport to Spanish Bay is in Monterey, California. Instead, the individual landed in Monterrey, Mexico. Even though this was pre-9/11, the booking agent and the carrier screwed up royally. He missed most of the event. The third story happened in Wentworth, England. I was golfing with my London employees but was very intimidated by the first hole. The tee box was right next to a long practice putting green. There must have been two hundred people on the putting green. Unable to block out the audience, I dribbled my drive.

The Finance Desk challenged the fixed-income sales force to a softball game. We had a ringer who worked for us who had played college baseball at North Carolina. Kip Schaefer was nothing short of brilliant. He was a superman. He hit homers, climbed fences, and threw out base runners, but it wasn't enough. I would like to say we let the sales force win for work's sake, but I'd be lying.

KEEPING UP TECHNOLOGICALLY

By the early 2000s, other dealers had developed and surpassed Vinny's computer system. Tim and I set out to build a state-of-the-art finance-trading platform. There were two ways to attempt this: in-house or out-of-house. Although the out-of-house option was cheaper and we were very comfortable with some of the players at the vendors, we were told we had to keep it in-house. Daniel O'Hara in Dublin was going to be the lead programmer, reporting to the head of fixed-income technology, Dan Rubin. I had been very impressed with Daniel on a trip years earlier. Although it was expensive and took a long time to build, it was going to be impressive. When Bear Stearns was taken over by JPMorgan Chase, the system was 95 percent complete. It never saw the light of day.

The repo market was the only market that remained operational all week during the 9/11 crisis. There was cooperation among the dealers, from the moment of the attack on America, who were competitors at any other time. Since Bear Stearns was located in midtown and its clearing bank was JPMorgan Chase, also located in midtown, we were very lucky. There were two clearing banks, JPMorgan Chase and Bank of New York (BONY). BONY was located downtown, and unfortunately, their backup site was also downtown. The power grid was destroyed. Both sites were inoperable although BONY tried to piece together their deliveries somehow. The entire process has now changed.

September 11 was on a Tuesday, and by Thursday of that week, Tim and I needed a break. The Finance Desk was on the fourth floor, so we walked down to the vacant equity trading area on the second floor. On the way we saw Ace Greenberg at his desk, making a few phone calls. Bear Stearns was his baby, and he didn't know what else to do to reassure people that Bear Stearns was OK.

After 9/11 the firm made a conscious decision to upgrade our disaster recovery (DR) site. A DR site is a small trading-floor setup for the entire firm away from the main area of business to be used in the event of an emergency to keep the firm viable. It was a short-term solution to a problem. The Finance Desk was a vital piece of the firm. We had to meet any challenge to survive. Without consciously trying, our desk was geographically diverse. We had people from Connecticut, Westchester, Long Island, New York, and New Jersey, and our DR site was in Whippany, New Jersey. Tim and I sent individuals out to Whippany every six months to make sure all the computers were up to date and to do a day of work from that location as practice. Fortunately, we never had to use our DR site, but a funny story happened there. Matt Chasin, our head mortgage trader, went out to Whippany one night for the next day's work. Because Matt wasn't familiar with the jughead turns in New Jersey, he got pulled over by a policeman for an illegal turn. He told the policeman that he was from out of town and here to do work at the Bear Stearns DR site. The officer said there were no DR sites in town. Matt had to drive him to the building. The officer was very surprised, and Matt didn't get a ticket.

WALL STREET CULTURE

We had a person on our desk named Fred Schweizer. Each Christmas he would hold a casual customer appreciation day at Morton's Restaurant in midtown Manhattan. This was attended by most of our New York customers and grew into a big event. He would go over around noon, and the rest of the desk would go after work. We called it "Fred-fest."

We created a one-time, new-business bonus commission each year for the sales force. The Finance Desk wanted new, consistent business. For any new repo customer, we would pay the salesperson two basis points for ninety days times their average balance. Although this cost us money each year, it got the sales force to focus on the Finance Desk product. In the first year of the new-business bonus commission only three sales people participated in it, by the end it was ten people. Since it was totally subjective and not accrued to the salesperson, I felt like the Pied Piper when I handed out the new-business bonus commissions each year to the sales force. It was distributed right before year-end when bonuses were decided, and they were especially appreciative.

SMDs had an A account. An A account was a glorified expense account given to each SMD to be used for a variety of purposes, including upgrading air travel, meal benefits, golf membership dues, and so on. It was several thousand dollars per year. Since we traveled very little, went out to dinner rarely, and had no golf memberships, we ate lunch like kings. A snowstorm was predicted during one winter in the early 2000s so our A team of ten people was staying in town at a hotel. Tim and I decided to take the team out for dinner. The bill came, and it was $1,400. We knew one of us was paying, but which one? We decided to try the "choose approach" from the Seinfeld TV show, and I lost.

In the early 2000s, Wall Street figured out a new way to make money. Many investors bought houses much bigger than they could afford. The only way to support them was through teaser rates. If the investor couldn't support that house at a normal thirty-year rate but could for three years or so at the teaser rate, they were gullible enough to try it. Another idea that factored into the financial crisis was the ability to make a AAA-rated security from a BBB-rated security. Wall Street would say 80 percent were AAA and the remaining 20 percent were below, so it equaled out to BBB. This 20 percent would be the first lost but the remaining 80 percent was not far behind (as we saw in the financial crisis). While mathematically it worked, intuitively it was wrong. The rating agencies agreed that 80 percent of these mortgages were AAA, and Wall Street packaged them in mortgage-backed securities. Investors saw a AAA security backed by an agency and bought in.

Shauna Richman was an A team member and had done a great job in prime brokerage. We had many fixed-income prime brokerage clients. They were profitable, and Shauna's team watched them like hawks. From a risk perspective, the most important item to monitor was their exposure. Many of the prime brokerage clients were hedge funds, and they were leveraged. This could work in a positive way but could also work in a negative way. Most owned mortgages, but some were positions that were in very hard-to-price instruments. We had several different ways to do the pricing. From basic feeds to matrix pricing to computer-generated models to trader pricing, we felt we were protected.

Trader pricing was the best. Later, I wasn't so sure trader pricing was the best because if we were asking them to price a security in a very illiquid market, they may have a conflicting viewpoint. If interest rates rose quickly or very unexpectedly, problems might occur.

If there was ever any question, we always looked at the most conservative price and made sure Bear Stearns was protected. Since Shauna's accounts were the most leveraged, they had to be closely monitored. We took margins on each security—the more esoteric, the bigger the margin. We rarely ever lost money. Shauna would come to Tim and me if there was a potential problem.

PERSONAL ISSUES

Pamela Horvath was Vinny's assistant. We didn't see her very much in our early years, but from what we did observe, our impression was she was as hard as nails. When Vinny left, she became our assistant. Contrary to our opinion, she was warm, well organized, and very efficient and a terrific asset to us. Pam became a great friend. As younger people on the desk got married, we went to receptions. Pam was usually invited and she loved to dance. She could always make the person she was dancing with look very comfortable. It showed me that having the right partner was paramount (both personally and professionally).

In 2007 I was diagnosed with primary lateral sclerosis (PLS). PLS is a very rare, progressive neurological disease affecting the upper motor neurons of a person. PLS affects voluntary muscles, such as in the hands, legs, and tongue. It is often confused with ALS which affects upper and lower motor neurons. PLS is about 1% of all ALS cases. Hence, PLS moves slower, it is debilitating, but not fatal. Work-wise, I relied on the members of the Finance Desk—Paul Friedman and especially Tim. I couldn't have asked for a better partner than Tim.

My third daughter played travel basketball for Darien. She was a very good player. Darien always played Norwalk every year. They were both strong teams. One time Darien lost a game by one point, and Meg became upset. She had missed a crucial foul shot near the end, although she'd scored twenty-six points and had been the star of the game. She did not see the big picture. Just like my trade in the beginning, she was only looking at one component. I learned to look at the overall spread in the book not just one particular trade. It was her overall game that counted—offense, defense, rebounding, and how well she made the other players perform—and not just that one foul shot. I have to keep reminding myself to take my own advice from my trade. It is important to look at your long term goals not just the immediate ones.

THE END OF BEAR STEARNS

When a customer could not provide adequate margin as is the case with extreme stress, we would sell out the security or securities he or she was financing with us. To meet the legal requirements of a "blowout", we would have to send a bid list out to at least three people and take the best price. Sometimes our trading desk was one of the bidders. There were some occasions that we might not get bids back, especially when the issues were small and the markets were moving fast. My most memorable blowout was when we sent bids out to five dealers and our own desk. Three never came back. On one security we got three prices: $80, $23, and $6. Blowouts weren't fun for anybody but especially not the client, who never agreed with our price and was watching years of hard work vanish in an instant.

In June 2007 the first bomb hit at work—Bear Stearns Asset Management (BSAM) imploded. BSAM was a small subsidiary of Bear Stearns. It had some equity mutual funds and a few fixed-income funds. To be completely transparent, the Finance Desk did no business with the fixed-income funds. Some fixed-income funds at BSAM contained all lower rated issues created by other dealers. So, although we were not technically involved, it had our name. BSAM had been allowed to grow way too big. Bear Stearns attempted to figure out the problem. Tim handled anything that came our way, and Bear Stearns survived.

Later that summer while I was in Hilton Head on vacation, I got a phone call from Tim, who said he had called almost the entire desk in on a Saturday to give reports to upper management. The reports were for a SEC meeting that Monday. The SEC wanted to make sure there was no contagion at Bear Stearns as a result of BSAM's "problem". The report was a snapshot look at the Finance Desk balance sheet. The SEC was impressed at Monday's meeting, and we used the reports going forward. I took the first plane home. Again, Bear Stearns had survived.

One of the downfalls of Bear Stearns was that there was very little change. New blood never came to Bear Stearns, through normal attrition or otherwise. Unlike most competitors, people rarely left Bear Stearns. This allowed the same people to remain at the top.

The big difference between investment banks and commercial banks was twofold: commercial banks had individual deposits (insured by the Federal Deposit Insurance Corporation) and access to the Federal Reserve window. The Federal Reserve window was used in emergency situations and provided the borrower with cash from the Federal Reserve. Investment banks did not have deposits or access to the Federal Reserve. There were five big US investment banks. Bear Stearns was the fifth biggest investment bank, behind Lehman, Merrill Lynch, Morgan Stanley and Goldman Sachs. Commercial banks had subsidiaries that were investment banks, but that was not the main purpose of the company.

BS15C3 was a very special account. As Bear Stearns had a big equity prime broker business, we had to set aside collateral to make sure their cash was secure. Since it was very time consuming, it was done each week. Our firm's best collateral was used to fund the money balances left at the firm by the prime brokerage clients. We had an SMD oversee this effort and an operations employee who was specifically assigned to this account and who communicated daily with the Finance Desk to make sure it complied every day. It would not have made a difference at the end, since many of the equity prime brokerage accounts took their money and left Bear Stearns, BS15C3 had our shortest Treasury collateral and a very large balance. We would have had a vastly lower weekly number that Tuesday. We were bought by JPMorgan Chase over the weekend, so it didn't matter.

On a daily basis, Bear Stearns borrowed more than usual—about 20 percent of our balance sheet was in the repo market. Although this was more than our peers, it was very profitable and Bear Stearns wanted to make as much as it could. In almost every environment, one could always make more money borrowing short rather than long (interest rates are lower but money is not "given" to you for a long period). In 2008 we saw a different scenario. Short-term money froze. The unsecured money that the firm was borrowing was no longer available creating a short term liquidity crisis. Our name was no longer solid. Although the repo desk was not the cause of the downfall, since we were the vehicle within the firm borrowing short term money, it was just a matter of time.

JPMorgan Chase, on the other hand, had absolutely no need for outside money. It had more than enough cash from its deposits. At the time of the merger, Bear Stearns' Finance Desk was borrowing about $125 billion, more than half daily; JPMorgan Chase had almost $1 trillion in deposits, most insured by the government. JPMorgan Chase knew us very well, as it had cleared our fixed-income position for years. We had several things that were very important to JPMorgan Chase: our equity prime brokerage unit and, more importantly, our building. The building was right next to JP Morgan Chase headquarters and was brand new. It was a valuable real estate to anyone but especially to them. In retrospect, Bear Stearns made mistakes but was the smallest of the "Big 5" investment banks. Lehman Brothers had nothing appetizing to others. John Thain sold Merrill Lynch to Ken Lewis' Bank of America. The remaining two—Morgan Stanley and Goldman Sachs—became bank holding companies in the fall of 2008, ending the era of the investment bank.

After Bear Stearns was sold to JPMorgan Chase, all banks, both investment and commercial, had access to the Federal Reserve, thereby allowing the Federal Reserve to be the lender of last resort. This may have saved Bear Stearns. Goldman Sachs and Morgan Stanley did not take retail deposits like other commercial banks but did take institutional deposits, which helped secure their equity base in case there was a run on their companies. They had some tough times, but did Hank Paulson, the Treasury Secretary and former CEO of Goldman Sachs, favor them while punishing Bear Stearns too much?

The end of Bear Stearns came in March 2008. It happened fast, and it was caused by a total lack of confidence in Bear Stearns by the investment community. We were the smallest of the big investment banks. The loss of confidence had very little to do with what we did; we were just too small. Our equity base could not support our balance sheet. JPMorgan Chase's equity base was far bigger than ours. They thought the mortgages that Bear Stearns owned were risky. Their claim was the mortgage position offset the value of other assets in the firm. Although they took over all the assets, they immediately moved their investment bank arm into our building. JPMorgan Chase bought Bear Stearns for $2 per share, later increased to $10 per share, despite our share price reaching about $170 a year earlier.

Caddying in upstate New York

Playing sports at Bucknell University

Members of the Finance Desk attending a colleague's wedding

Bear Stearns announcement of new Senior Managing Directors

Various golf events

Various golf events (continued)

Bear Stearns awarded #1 America's Most Admired Companies
– Securities Firm by Fortune (2002)

Golf with Bucknell Fraternity (FIJI) Brothers

Golf with Bucknell Fraternity (FIJI) Brothers (continued)

Awarding the Red Jacket and Trophy to winner of Annual Red Stackloaf Golf Tournament

Golf at the Lexus Champions for Charity

Dinner with Bear Stearns colleagues from NFL pool

LIFE

AFTER BEAR STEARNS

For the most part, JPMorgan Chase got rid of senior people. Tim and I would be fine financially—much better than we could have imagined more than twenty years before, despite losing a small fortune in Bear Stearns stock. We were the first casualty of the financial crisis, but not the last. Since the thirty-basis-point spread had not been there, I had not sold any short STRIPS. (This was selling the short strips verse converting some open reverses after the Joe Jett situation) I unwound my book in a week (it takes a while to close out $7 billion in trades) with many reconstitutions and a few strips. (I returned the STRIP pieces to the Federal Reserve and got the note/bond back. I would then return the note/bond back to the entity I had borrowed it from.) The unwind happened exactly as I thought it would, and I was never asked any questions about the STRIP matchbook. For me, having to worry about my medical situation made the loss of the only place I had ever worked bearable. The hardest part was watching my Finance Desk associates deal with the loss of their home away from home. The demise of Bear Stearns was not their fault, but they were the casualties. Most of our desk employees were paid very well, but they were relatively young and had not had time to build a nest egg. They all found jobs.

In March 2008 JPMorgan Chase coveted one of my fellow employees, a retail account executive named Steve Smith. Steve had a large position of government agencies and I worked with him daily on these positions. I wanted Steve to transition smoothly to JPMorgan Chase. I was scheduled to leave in May, so I turned to Ace Greenberg to try and extend my stay so I could facilitate the transition. I stayed until August. Steve went to JPMorgan Chase, and I filed for disability.

At the end, I wanted to talk to everyone on the desk and a few others about my PLS diagnosis. The people on the desk knew something was different with me but had no specifics. It wasn't a fun talk for me, but I wanted them to know.

After Bear Stearns disappeared, there were two personal things I had to do. The first was to find a new gym. The second was to follow through on my long-term disability policy. Since there was a gym at work, I had always been able to stay in shape, and after my diagnosis, I was able to do many exercises there. I had worked with a personal trainer twice per week, as well. Now, I didn't have that. Fortunately, I found Darien Physical Therapy. One of my doctors recommended a physical therapist there, and in addition, the office had a small gym and a trainer, Martin Ragonese, who stretched me. It became my home three days per week. I rode a stationary bike, lifted weights, and used all their facilities. It was perfect. Every night for years, I have stretched myself. Stretching is key to slowing PLS.

The second item proved to be much more difficult. I had taken out a supplemental disability policy through Bear Stearns' carrier. All the Bear Stearns benefits, including my primary and supplemental disability, were going away on September 1, 2008. They became JPMorgan Chase benefits. After filing for disability, I provided the carrier access to my medical records. After several conversations with the carrier, I received a letter denying my claim. I couldn't believe it. Now I was in a battle with Bear Stearns' carrier. It required serious action. I hired a lawyer, who, among other things, was a disability claims legal expert. I filed an appeal of the decision denying coverage as well as for disability with the Social Security Administration. In April 2009 the Social Security Administration approved my disability application. In May Bear Stearns' carrier approved my disability retroactively to November 2008 after they agreed with my appeal.

I learned there was a three-month period between filing date and the actual date an insurance policy took effect. Since I filed on August 15, my disability payments started on November 15. Bear Stearns' internal policy was to pay the health insurance premiums for disabled employees for life; JPMorgan Chase's was not, but they honored Bear Stearns' policy. Although I will be forever grateful to JPMorgan Chase for allowing my family to stay on its medical policy, I have to pay the monthly premiums. By staying that extra time (from May to August) to ensure Steve made it over to JPMorgan Chase, I was not eligible for the Bear Stearns policy, which was free health care for life.

I had, and still have, three doctors. The first is Dr. Amiram Katz, a neurologist in Orange, Connecticut, affiliated with Yale University, who specialized in Lyme disease. (Before I was diagnosed with PLS, I had the hope that my problems stemmed from Lyme disease.) The second is Dr. Hiroshi Mitsumoto, a neurologist and world-renowned doctor in the ALS field. He is the director of the Eleanor and Lou Gehrig MDA/ALS Research Center of the Neurological Institute of New York at Columbia University Medical Center. These two brilliant men look at my neurological problem from completely different directions. My third doctor is Dr. Debra Adler-Klein. Although PLS was out of her spectrum, she was a great sounding board for the varied recommendations I received. I saw each of them every three months (and still do, although Dr. Lynn Morris took over for her colleague Dr. Adler-Klein). In October 2014 I switched to Dr. Julia Voytovich. It was important to me to have a team of doctors. Several years before, a fraternity brother had died prematurely from a liver ailment. I wanted to make sure I had all the information to make my treatment decisions.

Before my diagnosis, I had to take an EMG test. It was barbaric. It hadn't changed that much since the Lou Gehrig days. There were two parts. First, they hooked me up to a computer to see how fast an electric current traveled through me. My "favorite" was when they tested the current from my neck to the tip of my finger. The second part consisted of sticking a needle equipped with a microphone into my muscles to see if they made a sound. Healthy muscles are silent, while muscles with neurological problems are not.

Dr. Katz had me take an antibiotic intravenously. If it was Lyme disease, this would take care of it. A visiting nurse came to my house each week for three months to change the line. I gave the antibiotic to myself intravenously every day. Even if it wasn't Lyme disease, Dr. Katz had seen some similar neurological cases and thought this might help me. Since then, I have been taking oral antibiotics twice per day. Dr. Katz thinks this medicine is helping me, while Columbia is skeptical.

Jim, a physical therapist at Darien Physical Therapy thought walking backward might help me. I never thought much of people who walked backward at the gym, but I gained a new appreciation for them. Walking backward fools the mind.

In early 2009 I began to get deep-muscle massages every other Thursday at Darien Physical Therapy. The doctors didn't think it would help my PLS, but the masseuse thought it would relax my muscles and allow the nerve connections to flow at their optimum. I thought it felt good, and now I go every week.

During my visits to the various neurologists, they had me perform tests. One was tapping my feet; the other was snapping my fingers. I figured if they were testing me, I might as well practice and get good at them. Since 2011 I have been practicing my tapping and snapping weekly at Darien Physical Therapy.

In the fall of 2009, my wife told Dr. Adler-Klein that I wasn't sleeping the same way. Upon hearing this, Dr. Adler-Klein immediately set up a visit with Dr. Roca at the sleep center at Stamford Hospital. When I saw him, he arranged an overnight sleep study at the hospital. I was hooked up to electrodes and went to sleep there one Friday night. The results showed I had sleep apnea. I'd always thought of big, overweight men with burly necks who snored a lot as sleep apnea candidates. I was not a big, overweight man, but I did sleep on my back and snore some. Little did I know, there are two types of sleep apnea: obstructive and central. Obstructive is the one I talked about but central comes from the nervous system, and there is no cure for it. Unfortunately, I have a combination of both. I now wear a full face mask at night. This mask blows air down my throat to make sure I breathe when asleep.

THE DISCOVERY

PLANNING AHEAD

My wife and I wanted to be very conservative with our children's college education. We wanted nothing left to chance. Although no investment is 100 percent risk free, we thought the federal government was the safest investment. As I said previously, we bought STRIPS for our children's college education—some in their UGMAs (Uniform Gift to Minors Act) and some in our joint account. We also bought additional STRIPS in case of further education. Needless to say, we had about twenty purchases of issues maturing over fifteen consecutive years (2009 to 2024). I will only talk extensively about the first one, but the same is true for each STRIP I bought thereafter. I paid the interest tax for every issue each year. Several issues have matured, and others have several years to maturity. I will provide numerical facts and some minor assumptions for the 8/15/2016 STRIP to show how this problem exists for all STRIPS, not just the 8/15/2009 STRIP.

I picked August for the maturity of the STRIPS so they would mature right before each year of college and pay for that year of school. The tax assumption I made was as follows: I would pay the unearned interest each year.

Before I go step by step through the 8/15/2009 STRIP that I bought, it is very important to understand original issue discount (OID).

STRIPS have no interest payment, but the holder must still pay taxes on the unearned interest. OID is the unearned interest that the holder pays taxes on each year. The investor receives a 1099 form from his or her brokerage firm. In my case, I was given the OIDs on a 1099, first from Bear Stearns and then from Fidelity Investments. The brokerage firm is given the OID for each issue by the Treasury Department, which uses a formula, and then the brokerage firm gives them to the investor on a 1099. The investor puts what he or she receives from the 1099 on his or her tax return. This figure is corroborated by the IRS. In the most recent government's OID brochure, there is a statement that says if the investor does not believe his or her 1099 is correct, it is the investor's responsibility to change it. Although this is definitely the case now, I am not sure it was in 1991 but in either case I just used what was on the 1099 and was never questioned on it. Arguably, this is contrary to what every investor believes to be true. If the 1099 is wrong, either fix it or don't give it out - but the Treasury Department has done neither.

In my opinion, investors in STRIPS are long-term holders. They invest in STRIPS for a date far in the future. They are normally retail or retail-like customers. The investor has no reason to believe the yearly "unearned interest" they receive for tax purposes is incorrect, either in the first year they buy it or the last year they own it or at any time in between.

This is where I have a very unique circumstance that led me to believe something was wrong. At Bear Stearns I had all my positions in one account, therefore I got one 1099. At Fidelity, due to my PLS medical condition and to make full use of the then tax laws, I separated the one account into several, isolating the education accounts (STRIPS). It was at this point that I received multiple 1099's every year. I put the 1099's on my taxes each year.

THE PROBLEM

I first noticed a problem while doing my taxes in March 2010. The 8/15/2009 STRIP I bought for my daughter, Katie, eighteen years earlier had matured. The Treasury paid me $35,000 on 8/15/2009, the face value, while I originally purchased the STRIP on 12/2/1991 for $8,363. The various OIDs I paid over the years on my taxes totaled $17,832. (The OID given to me by Fidelity Investments for 2009 was just $66.93.) This adds up to $26,195, which is a difference of $8,805 (35,000-26,195). I was never asked to pay taxes for unearned interest of $8,805. My issue should be easy: a STRIP held to maturity (principle plus interest).

Because of my extensive professional experience with STRIPS and my increasing personal interest due to my children's pending college educations, I analyzed them. I built a spreadsheet for every STRIP I owned. My guess is the average length held is twenty years, but let's assume eighteen years. If the federal government didn't collect interest of $8,805 on my $35,000 position, the amount of uncollected interest on a $200 billion market must be in the billions. What I discovered was unbelievable.

I thought I would bring it to the federal government's attention and it would gladly pay me a fee. I thought PLS research would benefit greatly. I was sure it would work. I was wrong.

The IRS issues publication 1212 (the IRS guide to OID). The primary purpose of IRS publication 1212 is to help brokers and middlemen identify publicly offered original discount (OID) debt instruments they may hold as nominees for the true owners, so they can file form 1099-OID or form 1099-INT as required. The publication goes on to say if the investor disagrees with the 1099-OID given to them, the investor is ultimately responsible. But what I do not understand is why the Treasury sends out any information to the brokerage firm and the brokerage firm sends that out to the investor. If the investor realizes that they should change every strip OID given to them and every 1099 sent to them is wrong, then why send them anything at all?

The IRS seeks to hold individual investors accountable for all tax issues relating to OIDs, notwithstanding their receipt of inaccurate information from brokerage firms and thus inaccurate information from the Treasury. The federal government must know that with such a faulty system, some investors pay tax on the appropriate interest, but most do not.

Several other factors exacerbate this problem:

1. There is only one line per 1099 on the tax form. If a person owns multiple STRIPS and changes the interest on one STRIP, how does the IRS know which one was changed?
2. Since the vast majority of STRIP holders use accountants and they download the 1099 straight from the brokerage firm, if there is an incorrect OID reported on the 1099, they will probably never know.

During a phone call with the IRS, their answer was they are only responsible for the collection of taxes. If investors do not agree with their 1099, they can change it. Regardless of another part of the US Treasury supplying incorrect OIDs, potentially costing the Federal Government billions of dollars, if investors use the supplied 1099 figure and not resort to their own calculations, the IRS is satisfied and will never question it.

I have had correspondence with the government, but it has fallen on deaf ears. It has happened with both Republican and Democratic administrations, so I don't think it is political. Since the amount of the US deficit has risen, by issuing greater amounts of notes and bonds, the STRIPS market has also risen, magnifying the issue. My guess is it started at the inception of the STRIPS program. Over the life cycle of STRIPS, the OID may balance out, but being a former trader, I know we cannot look at an issue over a life cycle. We have been in a low interest rate environment from inception and a dramatically lower interest rate environment since 2008. In the short term nothing is going to balance out.

If the federal government cannot understand the tax repercussions of OID, it should not try to estimate them for a 1099. When rates rise and therefore the OIDs rise investors will be charged too much. They may make the federal government alter its procedure. Until then, the government will lose out (and has already lost out) on significant tax revenue. The IRS uses publication 1212 as its fallback despite a 1099 being sent to investors by a reputable brokerage firm each year, stating what amount to pay. The federal government thinks they are right, the brokerage firms think they are right, and the investors think they are right. They are all wrong.

This is gross mismanagement by the US Treasury, which is costing the federal government vast sums of money in lost tax revenue. Without question, investors trust the figures provided to them in 1099s. The information provided by the government is 100 percent wrong. If investors are "forced" to use the formula in publication 1212, I have full faith it will be correct but by giving the investor an interest amount on a 1099, it provides an OID figure that investors rely on to pay taxes. It has cost and will continue to cost the US government billions of dollars. The IRS verifies that investors use the information given to them by brokerage firms. In a time where people talk about revising the tax code, let's just get this one right. The time is now!

HOW DID I CALCULATE
MY NUMBERS?

In the past I made some assumptions, but if anything they were too conservative.

1. My earlier estimate was from my own experience and used eighteen-years held (the time I bought them until the kids went to college). That is wrong. It is not just the period that I held them but from when the STRIP was created. From the Treasury's point of view, we have to use the length of the program (it started in 1985), since thirty-year bonds were in the program, and 120 coupons were always eligible from 160 issues (the coupons from the ten-year note are eligible but already in the thirty-year bond). The numbers are higher if we add in the principals, which are approximately an additional 160 issues, but let's just work with the coupons. I believe principals are treated the same way as coupons for tax reasons, and the amount of the principal maturing can just be added to the coupon maturing in February, May, August, and November of each year. The size of the market is larger than just my coupon maturing, especially when we add in the principals. The OID currently given out on every coupon

is wrong, and with rates very low, the difference is big, and as you get closer to maturity, the discrepancy is very large. That is why the discrepancy has been very high for the last several years and will continue to be. I will try to use my experiences as a barometer for estimating the lost revenue. The current market is approximately $200 billion. There are four payments per year, in February, May, August, and November. I assume the error is not just on the August issue but on all the coupons equally. There are a few other issues stripped, but they are small and immaterial. There are state, agency, and corporate issues as well, but I was never involved, so I can't comment on these. My guess is they are substantial and also wrong. I am just concentrating on Treasury STRIPS, but that is likely not the whole problem.

2. In my example, there was a total cost (including interest over eighteen years) of $26,195. This is a difference of $8,805 on a $35,000 STRIP held to maturity (8/15/2009). If we simply make the eighteen-year error a twenty-four-year error (2009-1985) to determine overall error size, the new total is $11,740. If the market is now $200 billion, let's assume it grew as follows. My professional experience has the market bigger in the beginning and then more stagnant, but let's assume this conservative pattern:

Year	Size	Year	Size	Year	Size	Year	Size
1985	25 billion	1994	140 billion	2003	165 billion	2012	192 billion
1986	50 billion	1995	145 billion	2004	168 billion	2013	196 billion
1987	75 billion	1996	145 billion	2005	171 billion	2014	201 billion
1988	85 billion	1997	145 billion	2006	174 billion	2015*	208 billion
1989	95 billion	1998	150 billion	2007	177 billion	2016*	215 billion
1990	105 billion	1999	153 billion	2008	180 billion	2017*	222 billion
1991	115 billion	2000	156 billion	2009	183 billion	2018*	229 billion
1992	125 billion	2001	159 billion	2010	186 billion	2019*	236 billion
1993	135 billion	2002	162 billion	2011	189 billion	so on*	

*Estimates

The average size of the market for my 8/15/2009 STRIP was $183 billion (2009) + $115 billion (1991) = $298 billion / 2 = $149 billion (average) / 120 (eligible coupons) = approximately $1.2 billion for that issue. With the average loss of $11,740 on a $35,000 position, the loss on that issue alone would be $11,740/$35,000 * $1.2 billion = $403 million over its life. If we multiply by the four payments that year, we get approximately $1,612 million. Interpolating that figure for approximately the size of market in a given year (year/149) * 1,612. For example, 1990 would be 105/149 * 1,612 million = $1,136 million; 2000 would be 156/149 * 1,612 million = $1,688 million; and 2019 would be 236/149 * 1,612 million = $2,553 million. As the market size gets larger, it compounds the error, which is why I think the error may be much larger. Again, these are only estimates based on my 2009 loss. The next five years would be greater, since the market size is greater. These conservative calculations through 2013 result in $45 billion in lost revenue by the federal government. I estimate from 2014 to 2019, an additional $14 billion will be lost.

3. Using the federal government's methodology, the price a person pays for a STRIP on the purchase date (in my example, $8,363) should be equal to the amount already collected as interest by the IRS. Since I can't go back and get those records, they are probably short. The IRS did collect something. Although the OID numbers appear to be better when rates are higher, this is difficult to quantify, and the market was smaller. Since traders used Yield to Maturity (YTM), the losses by the federal government were realized at that time.

4. The billion-dollar OID problem seems to be really exaggerated when interest rates are low. My 8/15/2009 interest expense was only $67, and my subsequent OID charges have also been low. This is completely counterintuitive to the last payment being the highest, since the principal is the greatest if held to maturity.

From the Treasury's point of view, every issue is at maturity when it comes due, whether it has been held by one investor or many. The interest expense should be the greatest if the issue is held for a long period. The last few years will have the greatest discrepancy. So 2009 was a substantial loss, but 2010 to 2014 was a real significant loss. An estimate of $45 billion in lost tax revenue could be on the low side.

5. As I said above, when an investor does not compute his/her OID but the 1099 is used, the 1099 is under estimates when interest rates are low. Interest rates will be extremely low through 2016 and historically low from 2017 to 2019 (per the Federal Reserve). $14 billion in future tax losses may be a low estimate.

ANOTHER EXAMPLE

The 8/15/2016 STRIP acts similarly to the 8/15/2009 STRIP. Looking at my spreadsheet, I purchased two lots: 65,000 STRIPS in Meg's account in 1996 for $15,626 and 70,000 STRIIPS in 2005 in our joint account for $42,335. There are several things that are unique to these purchases. The OID is at the same ratio each year (65/70), showing that there was one OID given per issue, regardless of purchase date. The second thing that is very apparent is that as the STRIPS market size has increased, the OID issue is larger. I will show you exactly how.

The OIDs and the purchase price on the sixty-five thousand purchase of 8/15/2016s in Meg's account totals $42,381 (I conservatively estimated the OIDs in 2014, 2015, and 2016); other OID assumptions could make the problem even worse. The OIDs and the purchase price on the seventy thousand 8/15/2016s in our joint account total $55,942. The sixty-five thousand is held for twenty years and has a differential of $22,619. If we use thirty years, the difference is $33,930. If we use the market size in 1996 of $145 billion and the market size in 2016 of $215 billion, the average is $180 billion. If we divide $180 billion by 120 coupons, this equals $1.5 billion per coupon as opposed to $1.2 billion, a 25 percent increase. So, the loss is $33,930/65,000 * 1.5 billion = $783 million. The year would be 4 * 783 million = $3,132 million. This is almost

$800 million higher than my assumption with the 2009 STRIP using a 3 year shorter period, a loss of $19 billion for the 2014 to 2019 period.

The second purchase happened in 2005, a shorter OID time frame, but still large and brings to light an additional problem. The seventy thousand is held eleven years and has a differential at maturity of $14,058, using the same conservative assumptions with the 65/70 ratio. If one uses thirty years, the difference is $38,340. Since the STRIP was only bought in 2005, the market size is even greater. If we divide the 193 billion by 120 coupons, the average size has now increased from 1.5 billion to about 1.6 billion. If we multiply $38,340/70,000 * 1.6 billion, the OID interest loss resulting from the under collection of taxes is $876 million. Multiply by four coupons, and the loss for that year is $3.5 billion, a far larger amount than my 2009 estimation of $2.3 billion and a shorter maturity (2016 vs. 2019). In my experience, as the market size increases, the issue gets worse. The federal government realizes some of the loss at the closer date (2005).

The 2016 scenario provides an even bleaker picture then my 2009 example (A loss of $19 billion not $14 billion). And, both scenarios only take into account OIDs within a 5 year time frame – as opposed to the entire 30 year OID period.

Presently, the interest rate environment is low and expected to remain low as well as the continued vast issuance of debt by the government resulting in the expansion of the STRIP marketplace. The federal deficit, now approaching $18 trillion, makes the government's loss in tax revenue from STRIPS even more staggering and bewildering.

WHAT NEEDS TO BE DONE

How should the government correct its long-standing miscalculations and inaccuracies in taxing in the $200 billion STRIPS market? I think this is a two-pronged effort for the U.S. Treasury and the Internal Revenue Service.

U.S. Treasury

1. Stop supplying the OID.
2. Force brokerage firms to supply the correct information on their 1099 using the publication 1212 formula. They "know" what their clients own. Provide "past" years with sample 1212 verse OIDs given on 1099s.
3. Brokerage firms should supply a new cost basis for every STRIP held by investors every year.

Internal Revenue Service

4. Recoup three years of unpaid back taxes from investors who relied on inaccurate OIDs from 1099s (approximately $6 billion).
5. Correct the outstanding issues and collect the correct taxes owed.

6. As the issue matures, have a "true up" line on a tax form to correct the many years of incorrect reporting.
7. All income is ordinary income and needs to be made whole at maturity. Capital gains or losses should only be on issues held and traded before maturity. The purchase price and the interest (over a STRIPS life) needs to equal the amount paid by the government at maturity.

In summation, if the investor relies solely on the 1099 given to him, one which is corroborated by the IRS, does not calculate a new OID pursuant to a formula contained in publication 1212, the investor is not paying the appropriate taxes. The brokerage firms know the STRIP issues their customers own. Give them the correct OID interest figure on the 1099. The brokerage firm should provide what the calculation is from 1212 to the investor. Currently, the government makes it very easy to make this mistake by providing a figure to the brokerage firms so they can give an incorrect figure on a 1099 and not "force" the investor to use 1212. By using this method it is costing the Federal Government billions.

LIFE CONTINUES

NEW PARTNERS

I now see a physical therapist, Mike Morgan, three times per week at Darien Physical Therapy. On Monday and Friday, I work on balance issues; on Wednesday, I work on stiffness. Recently, as the PLS has progressed, I have been getting headaches. This happens when I am a passenger in a car and my head is jostled through normal driving or if I have to turn my head for an extended time. Mike tries to alleviate these headaches by massaging my neck muscles. Recently, I have been headache free: for now, a problem solved.

When I go to our cottage in Chatham, I have to keep up my regimen of stretching, lifting, and so on. Fortunately, I found the Chatham Health and Swim Club. It is owned and managed by Carol Penfield. I lift and swim whenever I am there. Marina Brock has been instrumental in providing assisted stretching for me. Like having multiple doctors, it is always great having multiple opinions from the people who stretch me often.

Whenever I try to do two things (such as walking and talking), which I used to take for granted, I can't. My trainer at Darien Physical Therapy has been working with me to focus on just one thing; for example, turning the voluntary body movement of walking into an involuntary movement. I move slower but look normal. There is no standard way to treat PLS, but this idea has helped me.

In 2013, under the direction of Dr. Richard Mayeux, chairmen of the Department of Neurology at Columbia, the Neurology Advisory Council (NAC) was formed. I was asked to be on it along with my sister, Beth. This volunteer group was created to build public awareness for the Department of Neurology. Members of the NAC serve in an advisory and supportive capacity. This group of individuals brings a wide range of professional and personal expertise, providing input to the Department of Neurology and helping to keep it at the forefront of neuroscience.

Until a person has a need for a neurologic doctor, he or she doesn't think much about it. Problems in the brain are now affecting many in more numerous ways (NFL settlement, children playing football, soccer, or other sports at an early age and getting concussions). From ALS to Alzheimer's to Parkinson's to Multiple Sclerosis to Muscular Dystrophy to many others, neurologic issues will only become more frequent as the population grows and survives to an older age.

DIFFERENT CHALLENGES

In 2011 Matt Mondeaux, a resident of Buffalo, decided to raise money and awareness for ALS and the Eleanor and Lou Gehrig MDA/ALS Research Center of the Neurologic Institute of New York at Columbia University Medical Center. He intended to walk from his home to Yankee Stadium (about 500 miles) in a vintage Lou Gehrig uniform to attend a game. I found out about his effort after he had begun and contacted the Yankees. I still had those season tickets. When they learned of Matt's endeavor, the Yankees brought him and his family onto the field, as well as Dr. Mitsumoto and his wife to announce the achievement. They had seats for them. Regina Youngman, a nurse practitioner at Columbia, and her family used my seats to enjoy the festivities.

Recently, the ice-bucket challenge has brought awareness and funds to ALS research. Since PLS is on the ALS spectrum, it should be a beneficiary.

A few years ago, I was the first person in the COSMOS trial being run at Columbia University Medical Center. It included several other hospitals and was an ALS and PLS study. There were only thirty-nine PLS cases during the collection period; two and a half years, and all were used, as well as a sample of fifty ALS cases. These cases were given a partial DNA sequencing. They were looking to see if there was any genetic linkage. I was found to have a genetic abnormality. I have a problem in the *SPG7* gene. This is the spastic gene, and it was hetero-zygote. This means I have only one chromosome where I should have two. The good news is that this gene cannot be passed on to my children. Dr. Mitsumoto talked to Dr. Fink (another neurologist and an expert in genetics) at the University of Michigan. He thought I might have a problem with my muscle mitochondria. In November 2013 I had a muscle biopsy done to look for red ragged fibers in my left quadriceps. There were none.

My PLS is progressing, and my control is getting worse. I don't have the fight I used to have. If not for going to Darien Physical Therapy, I know I would be much worse. Needless to say, I don't play golf any-more. I have a walker for around the house and a wheelchair for long distances, and my speech is much slower, but I am still better than most.

EPILOGUE

FINAL THOUGHTS ABOUT STRIPS

It has been over six years since Bear Stearns was swallowed up by JPMorgan Chase. I am sure it is a Harvard Business School example. I no longer have to think of Bear Stearns every moment, but I do think about it occasionally.

Several things cross my mind: Could my signature STRIP trade, understanding all the nuances, be used by different departments? Since a borrow/pledge has equal dollar amounts, as rates fell over long periods of time, was there an advantage to my trade? Can stripping or reconstituting certain issues create a trading advantage? If an issue's price was at a premium to par, how could breaking it up produce every item at a discount?

I think about the tax ramifications every time one of my STRIPS matures or I pay taxes. As the market for STRIPS continues to grow, I cannot help but believe that the federal government continues to lose billions of dollars in tax revenue.

LIVING WITH PLS

In the fall of 2008, with the help of Bill Michaelcheck, Paul Friedman, and, most importantly, Charlene McKay, Paul Friedman's assistant, I sent a letter to my former Bear Stearns colleagues to raise money for PLS research. It was a very difficult time to be asking these former employees for money. They responded with tremendous generosity. I raised approximately $175,000.

The Spastic Paraplegia Foundation is a charitable organization formed to find a cure for PLS and HSP (hereditary spastic paraplegia). HSP is a rare disease that is also an upper motor neuron disease. It is genetic and affects a person's gait. I began to attend the annual meeting and found out several things. HSP, though rare (15,000 people in the US), is much more common than PLS (1,500 people in the US). Although there is no standard treatment for PLS, the physical therapy sessions, assisted stretching, light weightlifting, swimming, massage, multiple doctors, and my nightly stretching appears to have helped me. I diligently follow this regimen. It seemed like 80 to 90 percent of the people who attended the conference and had PLS were in wheelchairs. I was in the best condition by far.

I have a one of a kind viewpoint, being a patient and a long-time advocate of research. As a patient, I know the grace and dignity which Columbia has treated me with over the years. I have been to many annual SPF conferences so I have seen other PLS patients up close and continue my regimen because I am definitely better than most. As a member of the Neurologic Advisory Council, I see brilliant doctors, impressive research, and a desire to conquer all neurologic diseases including PLS. In my opinion, Columbia University Medical Center combines the best research with care. That is why all proceeds from this book are going to PLS research. Again, if a reader wants to make a tax-deductible donation to help fund PLS research, I would be most appreciative. Kindly make checks payable to The Trustees of Columbia University, indicate David S. Marren PLS Research Fund on the memo line, and mail to the following address:

Columbia University Medical Center
Office of Development
Attention: Matt Reals
100 Haven Avenue, Suite 29D
New York, NY 10032

As you know, I have four children. Katie spent her college days at Vanderbilt and is now attending Cornell Law School. Molly and Meg attend Caroline's and my alma mater, Bucknell University. Peter is at Darien High School. STRIPS have paid for all their higher education. With the cost of a 4 year private college for Peter approaching $300,000, it was easier investing a fraction of that cost in STRIPS and letting the security grow over 18-20 years. College comes faster than you think. STRIPS were the ideal security to pay for college. I think it may be for many families.

The best decision I ever made was in July 1988, to marry Caroline. She has been a partner in all my decisions and has been with me every step of the way.

After I was diagnosed in 2007, I would often go to the Darien YMCA to swim. My son, Peter, was in Little League. All I wanted was to see him hit a home run over the fence. It kept me going. When he was twelve, he hit eight homers over the fence. Maybe with your help I can do the same for PLS research.

Through faith and devotion I have added

Photo Courtesy: Joe Vericker – St. Patrick's Cathedral, New York 9/2015

a new member to the team.

Photo Courtesy: Servizio Fotografico – Vatican City, Italy 10/2015

REFERENCES

"Instruments Discount (OID) Issue Original Guide," accessed May 1, 2013, www.irs.gov/pub/irs-pdf/p1212.pdf.

"Whistleblower Protection Act," *Wikipedia*, last modified September 7, 2014, http://en.wikipedia.org/wiki/Whistleblower_Protection_Act.

"Who/What are Primary Dealers?" US Department of the Treasury, last modified December 7, 2010, http://www.treasury.gov/resource-center/data-chart-center/quarterly-refunding/Pages/primary-dealers.aspx.

"Zero-coupon bond," *Wikipedia*, last modified December 6, 2014, http://en.wikipedia.org/wiki/Zero-coupon_bond.

Made in the USA
Middletown, DE
19 November 2016